CHOICES

A journey of loss, life, justice, and forgiveness

By
Tiki Finlayson
Speaker, Co-Founder of 1N3

CHOICES by Tiki Finlayson
Copyright © 2023 by Bush Publishing & Associates

ISBN/SKU Paperback: 978-1-944566-43-2

ISBN/SKU Ebook: 978-1-944566-44-9

All rights reserved. No part of this book may be reproduced, stored in a retrieval system or transmitted in any form or by any means, electronic, photocopied, recorded or otherwise, without the prior permission in writing of the publisher, except for the use of brief quotations in a book review. For more information, contact Bush Publishing & Associates, LLC.

Any internet addresses, phone numbers, or company or product information printed in this book are offered as a resource and are not intended in any way to be or imply an endorsement by the publisher, nor does the publisher vouch for the existence, content, or services of these sites, phone numbers, companies, or products beyond the life of this book.

First printing 2023 by Bush Publishing & Associates, LLC., Tulsa, Oklahoma

www.bushpublishing.com

Bush Publishing & Associates, LLC., books may be ordered at bookstores everywhere and at Amazon.com. For information contact: info@bushpublishing.com

Book Cover design by Derek Yates Photography
Printed in the United States of America.

Dedication

This book is dedicated to my son, Kevin. May your story live on forever and continue to change the lives of those who hear it. I will be your voice in this world. I am so proud to be your Momma! See you soon sweet boy.

Table of Contents

DEDICATION III
TABLE OF CONTENTS IV
PREFACE IX
CHAPTER 1   HOW DO I SAY GOODBYE 1
LETTER TO KEVIN 1

    A RUDE AWAKENING-DAY 1, JULY 31, 2011 1
    HOW I HEARD THE NEWS 3
    DOE BEH 6
    A FATALITY ON THE SCENE 8
    BED #12 AND NOW BED #4 10
    BAD DREAM TURNED INTO A NIGHTMARE 11
    WHEN TO SAY WHEN 12

CHAPTER 2   THE NEXT SEVEN 17

    STEPPING INTO A DIFFERENT REALITY-Monday, AUGUST 1, 2011 17
    GOING HOME WITHOUT KEVIN 18
    EXHAUSTED AND OVERWHELMED 20
    PLANNING MY BABY'S FUNERAL 21
    SURROUNDED BY CASKETS AND GRAVES 26
    HEARING ALL THE NOISE 29
    PLEASE DON'T MAKE ME OPEN MY EYES 30
    FIXING KEVIN'S HAIR 30
    THE VIEWING – ('PRE-PARTY') 32
    THE PARTY NO ONE WANTED TO ATTEND 33
    KEVIN'S LIFE CELEBRATION PARTY 34
    KEVIN'S LITTLE PIECE OF LAND 35

CHAPTER 3   A LIFE FOR A LIFE 39

    RECIPIENTS 41

    A BIRTHDAY CELEBRATION 42

    HEARING THE SOUND OF HIS HEART 45

    FINYATELLISONS 48

    MELVIN'S LETTER 49

    OTHER CARRIERS OF KEVIN 53

    HONORING KEVIN 53

    THANKS FOR GIVING CEREMONY 54

    ROSE PARADE 54

    DONATE LIFE TRANSPLANT GAMES OF AMERICA 57

    BECOME A SUPER HERO LIKE KEVIN.. 58

CHAPTER 4   ROAD TO RECOVERY 59

    DADDY WOKE UP 59

    QUARANTINED 60

    WHERE IS KEVIN 61

    GETTING CLOSURE WITH KEVIN DYING... 62

    DADDY'S NORMAL SELF 63

CHAPTER 5   JUSTICE AND MERCY 65

    JUSTICE FOR KEVIN 65

    LEGAL PROCESS 65

    FIRST COURT DATE 67

    SECOND COURT DATE 67

    THIRD COURT DATE -RESTORATIVE JUSTICE 68

    SENTENCING DAY 71

    IS THIS ALL KEVIN'S LIFE IS WORTH 73

    ASKING FOR RELEASE 75

    MY VICTIM IMPACT STATEMENT 76

    ONLY "HALF WAY" HOME 79

    590 DAYS... 79

CHAPTER 6 CHOICES MATTER 83
- LIFE SENTENCE 84
- CHOICES WE WERE FORCE TO MAKE 86
- THE CHOICE I WAS NOT FORCED TO MAKE 86

CHAPTER 7 GRIEF AND FORGIVENESS 89
- GRIEF THROUGH MY EYES 89
- A LITTLE SIDE NOTE 92
- FORGIVENESS PLAYS A ROLE IN HEALING GRIEF 94
- QUOTES 98
- WHAT FORGIVENESS IS NOT 99
- WHAT FORGIVENESS IS AND DOES 99
- UNFORGIVENESS 100

CHAPTER 8 1N3 101
- A MISSION IS BORN 101
- KEEPING MANGLED METAL 104
- TOW VEHICLE 104
- 1,629 DAYS 105
- HAVE AWARENESS WILL TRAVEL 105
- SHARING OUR 1N3 STORY 105
- OTHER 1N3 STORIES 106
- THEN THERE WERE TWO 107

CHAPTER 9 THE RIPPLE EFFECT 111
- ALICIA 112
- CASEY BROSTEK 117
- CASSIE NOEL 126
- CRYSTAL, Kevin's Aunt 129
- DIXIE RENE' BELL, Kevin's Mimi 132
- TALISA WALKER 136
- LATISHA STEPHENS 141

CHAPTER 10 COMING OUT OF THE FOG ... 145
- THEN AND NOW ... 145
- DAY 3,007 ... 145
- THE DARKROOM ... 146

CHAPTER 11 KEVIN HAS THE LAST WORK ... 149
- KEVIN DANIEL YATES ... 150
- LOVE ... 151
- SOAR ... 152
- THE SWEET, SWEET LOVE OF GOD ... 153
- LESS IS MORE ... 154
- BIBLE ... 155
- RESPECT ... 156
- PAIN ... 157
- BE ASSURED ... 158
- PRESSURE ... 159
- FAST ... 160
- GOD ... 161

ABOUT THE AUTHOR ... 163
ACKNOWLEDGMENTS ... 167
CONTRIBUTORS ... 168
NOTES ... 170

Preface

Have you ever had something happen in your life that you thought you would not survive, and the grief that it brought was as thick as fog and you couldn't see tomorrow? Have you ever experienced emotional pain to the point that your body hurt all over, and in the moment, the thought crosses your mind that you wanted to die?

This is where I found myself in July 2011. **My life was forever changed through one of the most unimaginable experiences life could have thrown at me. While** trying to figure out how to say goodbye to the life I had known, I reached for courage and strength to find the key to unlock the door and be free to live again. It was not an easy journey neither coming out of the fog nor walking through grief, loss, life, and justice into forgiveness and a life of motivating others to do the same. I did it with determination to change my world as well as those around me by making one choice after another.

To set the stage for CHOICES, I did not write this book as a chronological start to finish story. Instead, each chapter will reveal different parts of my journey since July 2011. It has taken me seven long, emotional years to see what the fog was hiding and put words on the pages of this book. While I felt this book was finally complete, this journey has not and will not end until I take my last breath.

In this book you will discover how your CHOICES matter, and how they impact those around you in a positive or negative way. You will find how one choice can change your whole life. Through the pages of this book you will learn there can be new life in loss, freedom in justice, and real forgiveness is within your reach no matter the circumstance. As you read CHOICES my hope is the words will encourage you to think before reacting in tough situations, and will inspire you to live your best life one choice at a time.

Now, come with me as I take you on a journey of CHOICES.

Chapter 1

How Do I Say Goodbye

LETTER TO KEVIN

<u>**A RUDE AWAKENING-DAY 1, JULY 31, 2011**</u>

DEAR KEVIN, MY SWEET BOY, this still doesn't seem real…. I remember being all alone running down the deserted hospital hallway early that Sunday morning, not knowing for sure where to find you. It seemed like a scene out of a horror movie as I ran. The hall got longer with every step. I was praying for you even though I didn't know exactly what had happened. I was wondering why you didn't call to tell me you had been in a car accident. It was a terribly helpless feeling to know my baby was lying in a hospital bed in pain and alone with no one you knew, there to comfort you.

It was surreal, like I was watching myself in a movie. I was in two places at the same time. I felt like I was both inside and outside of my body. As I finally burst through the door of Erlanger Emergency Room, there stood two police officers in the waiting room. On any other day it would have been full of people waiting their turn to be seen by a doctor. On this day it was eerily empty and quiet.

The officers asked if I was your mother. I said, "Yes, where is Kevin? I need to see him"! They asked me to follow them and walked me to the other side of the room. I just assumed they were taking me to see you. As they opened the door and we entered the room, you were not there! It was a private waiting room, and they told me someone was coming to talk to me about your injuries. A lady who worked in registration, named Anita, came through the door carrying a small manila envelope. She asked if I would sit down and handed it to me. It contained your Zelda wallet, blood stained dog tags with your gamer tag engraved "Algid Frost", your blue earring, and your cell phone. The phone was bent and the face cracked. (We later learned it was in your pocket and helped absorb the force of impact as your driver door was smashed and had pinned you in).

Anita proceeded to tell me how sorry she was and that she had been handed your belongings shortly after you arrived in the emergency room at 2:30 a.m. She said it had been unusually quiet through the night and into the morning so she began to pray as she was holding your phone. "God, please let this phone work so I can let this baby's family know where he is. He needs them here".

She tried everything to pull up a contact on your phone or to dial the last number you called. She said your phone kept ringing and doing all sorts of crazy things, but she could not answer it. By this time it was early morning around 7:00 a.m. She prayed one more time and said, "God, please have someone call this baby's phone and please let me be able to answer it". To her surprise at 7:10 a.m., your phone rang. She answered and heard, "You are not Kevin, where is he"? It was one of your friends, Phil. Thank God for Phil! If it had not been for him, who knows how long you would have been there before we were notified

HOW I HEARD THE NEWS

Phil worked third shift less than a mile from the crash scene. He was on his way home when he passed by and saw your mangled van in the grass off the side of the road. The officers were still working the scene six and a half hours after the accident. He thought to himself, "That looks too much like Kevin's van". At that point he didn't care if he woke you up. He called your phone to make sure it wasn't you. He said his stomach sank when he didn't hear your voice on the other end of the phone. He immediately drove to our house and noticed only one car there. After what seemed like an eternity while desperately banging on the door, Derek finally answered. He thought he was dreaming when he heard the news, but it was reality. You had been in a head-on collision. That was all Phil knew. By now it was almost 8:00 a.m. and it was left to Derek to make the horrible phone calls to tell the family.

Tom had left the house at 5:00 a.m. to drive back to Houston, Texas, and was already in Birmingham, Alabama. He turned around and headed back when he heard the news. I was where I had been for the past five days, sleeping in the Erlanger ICU Waiting Room, where your Pipi was in the ICU trauma unit still in critical condition. I was sleeping on the opposite end of the hospital while you were trying to hang on to your life, hooked to machines and tubes, going through what seemed like hundreds of scans and x-rays. You had been at the hospital for five and a half hours before I even knew you had been in a car accident. All of this had happened before I got the phone call.

I had been sleeping every night listening to music with my earbuds in to help drown out the noise of the ICU. My ringer on my phone was also music, so when my phone rang at 7:15 a.m., it didn't register with me that my phone was ringing. By the time I was awake enough to realize it, I had missed the call. It was from (423) 778-1234, I will never forget that number as long as I live. It was a hospital number and when I tried to call the number back it did not accept incoming calls. I immediately thought the call was from upstairs about my Daddy. I went over to use the hospital phone to call the nurse to make sure he was okay. He was, and they assured me that they had not called me. I was very bewildered about the phone call. It was Sunday and I knew the Administration Office was closed. Who had called me from a hospital number? I decided to just forget about it and went to brush my teeth and hair. That is where I was when I got the news. You had been there in the emergency room for hours with hospital staff and the trauma team working frantically to save your life...but you were alone.

So there I sat holding your personal belongings, listening to this lady tell me how she wasn't able to notify us. As she was talking, a dark haired man wearing scrubs entered the room holding a chart in his hand. He was a doctor. He begins to tell me the long list of injuries, as well as the severity of them, and that you had been taken to surgery to repair your left arm and both legs. Brain scans were being done while you were in surgery. He said they were doing all they could, but it didn't look good.

Again, I could see this whole thing playing out. It was as if I was sitting on the ceiling watching and hearing myself. In my mind, I was hysterical, crying and screaming, but what I was seeing myself do was entirely different. I heard myself say to the doctor, "I appreciate your ability and the knowledge God gave you, but I'm a believer. I've been through this with my pastor and my Daddy with head injuries. And if He can heal them, He can touch Kevin's brain and heal Kevin's brain. And whatever needs to be done with the rest of his body, I have complete expectation that Kevin is going to come out on top of this. We are in agreement. God said where two or three are gathered in agreement that it is done, so I'm expecting it done. However long it takes, it's going to be done. So you do what you know to do for him and I'll do what I know to do on this end." He thanked me and said he needed to go and take care of Kevin.

As I was signing the release for your belongings, your Dad

and Wendy came in and Derek came soon after. We were told to go wait in the same ICU waiting room where I had been for almost a week. As we made our way back across the hospital I kept thinking to myself, "This is a horrible dream! WAKE UP! This is not real!!!" When we got back to the waiting room, family and friends were arriving. Most had been getting ready for church when they received the news. Before long the waiting room was filled with people who love you. It was the longest four and a half hours of my life before getting to walk into the ICU and see you.

DOE BEH

When it was finally time to go up to see you it was 12:30 p.m. I had a lady from the hospital come and tell me you had to be identified first because you were admitted as "DOE BEH." They couldn't find your wallet in your pocket when you first arrived, so you were a DOE! (Why they didn't change it to "Kevin Daniel Yates" from what was on your driver's license, I have no clue.)

The lady proceeded to tell me that I had to prove I was your mother before they would let me identify you! I lost it at that point. You know how your Momma is, no one messes with my boys! I told her very strongly and adamantly, "You allowed me to sign for Kevin's personal belongings and I had no I.D. or proof of who I was on me, and now you're telling me I have to prove I am his mother!! How the hell do you expect me to prove it?!! Now let me see my son!!" She then decided it was not necessary for me to do that before seeing you.

I remember riding in the elevator with her and two officers, I really don't even remember who else was there. We walked through the winding hallway, past all the people who were waiting to see their loved ones. I had been one of them for the last five days waiting to see my Daddy in bed twelve. Now they all had to wait to see their loved ones so that I have to go in and identify you, my son, my Kevin, my Sunshine. As the double doors to the ICU trauma unit opened and I was escorted to bed four, it seemed the hallway kept getting longer and longer with every step. I was trying to prepare myself for whatever I was about to see. As we came to your room, there was a doctor shining a light in your eyes and two nurses, Renee and Jana, (who I now call my earth angels) in the room with clipboards, monitoring all the machines. I looked at you and said, "Yep, that's my baby."

Your sweet face was so swollen with stitches down your forehead, across your eyelid and down your cheek and you had a breathing tube in your mouth. Your long beautiful hair was tangled and matted with your blood and full of tiny slivers of glass. Your left arm and leg were both in a cast and your right leg in traction. I wanted so badly to crawl up in that bed and hold you. It didn't matter that you were twenty-five and six foot five inches tall. You were my baby boy and I wanted to make everything better. You hated pain. I wanted to fix it like the many other times in the past, but I couldn't. All I knew to do was pray and live what I believed.

Tom had finally made it back from Birmingham, Alabama. I was so glad to finally have him there with me; I knew he was upset too, because he loved you like a son. He stayed by my side, trying to be strong and there for me, even though his heart was broken for me and you. We would go in your room and I would stand at the left side of your bed, on your right side, which was not broken and gashed, and lean down and talk to you, with your Mimi by my side.

I knew you were not present in the room with us. Your body was there, but you were not. I would tell you that you had to come back, and for you to tell Jesus you couldn't stay and for Him to send you back. I told you that you had a life to live and I needed you to come back, you had things to do. All I would tell people was, "All is well with Kevin!" I wouldn't say anything else and wouldn't let anyone say anything different. I knew and believed that God was no respecter of persons and that He had raised others up from their deathbeds and He could do the same for you. I didn't want anyone's words or anything to hinder that.

A FATALITY ON THE SCENE

I kept trying to get answers as to what had caused the car accident. Why did this happen? How did we get here? It wasn't until about 4:30 p.m. that we knew anything about what even happened. We were originally told there was a fatality and we thought whoever was in the other vehicle in the accident had died. I had been praying for that family as well as ours. They had lost someone and you were still here, at least that is what I thought. Then we found out the truth. The driver of the vehicle that hit you was drunk and had gotten on the wrong side of the concrete barrier on a divided highway, and drove over four miles before hitting you head-on. She was alive. She was in the same hospital with injuries as well. Now there was a whole different set of circumstances to deal with. The "accident" had now become anything but. Anytime a person gets behind the wheel of a vehicle intoxicated it is NEVER an "accident"! It was now a collision, a crash, a wreck, due to someone making a stupid, senseless choice, committing a 100% preventable crime! The fatality that was said to be in the wreck was YOU. You died three times on the way to the hospital, but you were hanging on. And as I saw you laying in that hospital bed fighting for your life, I flashed back to the day you were born. You were born four weeks early. You had to be hooked up to all kinds of machines with tubes and IVs and had to spend the first week of your life in the NICU fighting for life. Now twenty-five years later, here we are again.

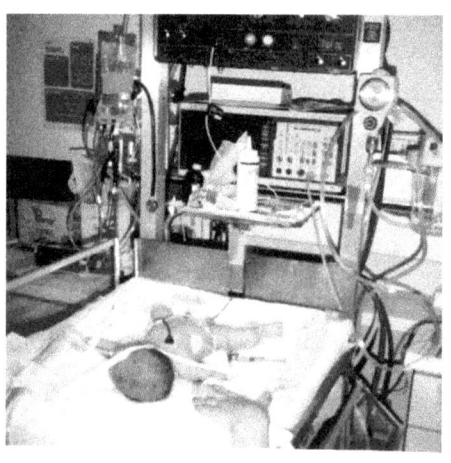

We were gathered in a small room just outside the TICU waiting room to be told how this horrible wreck happened. Again, it was still as though I was watching myself from up in the corner of the ceiling. I saw our family gathered in a circle, holding hands and praying. As I started to pray I heard myself say, "I forgive her for what she has done to our family. And if she doesn't know You, Lord, let me be the one to show her." As I watched all of this I couldn't believe what I heard myself say! Did I really say that out loud? Yes, I did! While some family members stood quietly in shock not sure what to say, others were angry, and as they stormed out of the room they said they couldn't believe I would do such a thing when you were lying in there fighting for your life. But for me personally, I needed my prayers to reach Heaven! Your life depended on it! I had to live what I believed.

BED #12 AND NOW BED #4

We were given permission to come and go in the TICU to be with you. There was a constant stream of family and friends coming to see you. Every time I went in I would tell you that you couldn't go and you still had things to do. I was very strong and adamant. I was determined that you were coming out of this. I wouldn't allow anyone to say anything any different in my presence. While all of this was going on in bed four with you, your Pipi was still in bed twelve. The family took turns rotating to see him and I would briefly make an appearance and then tell him I had to go and take care of some things. He had not spoken since he woke up two days prior, and as I was leaving he asked where I was going. Of all times for him to start to speak! Pipi's doctors had told us that we could not tell him what had happened to you due to his head injury. They were not sure what might happen or if it could cause a setback. It was hard to walk in with a smile when I was screaming and crying on the inside. So I quickly said to him, "I just have to check on some things and I'll be back next visit." I walked out of the room and cried as I walked down the hall, around the nurse's station, and just eight doors down to your room.

I kept thinking that I would wake up and this horrible nightmare would finally be over, but I never did. Finally, day turned to night. It had been a long, draining day and most everyone had gone home. I tried to settle into my usual spot in the ICU waiting room where I had been for the past five days and four nights. The only difference was now, not only did I have my Daddy still in critical condition, you were there too. I tried to sleep but it wasn't happening for me, so I prayed that you would improve through the night if we let you rest. Morning couldn't come soon enough for me to see you again.

BAD DREAM TURNED INTO A NIGHTMARE

We were called early and told there would be a meeting at 9:00 a.m. to talk with the doctor about you and to have the family there. At 8:45 a.m. everyone gathered in the small room again just outside the TICU. I was sure we would hear good news; that you had improved through the night. But instead the nightmare became worse. The doctor said, "This is the hardest part of my job. It is with deep regret that I tell you we pronounced Kevin "brain dead" at 8:57 a.m. and you should discuss the option of organ donation." I started screaming inside my head, "WAKE UP!!! WAKE UP!!!" But this was really happening . . . this was reality. However, I was not ready to accept those words. I told the doctor, "You CANNOT do that without my permission! And we are NOT talking to anyone about organ donation! I'm giving God all the time He needs to do whatever He is going to do!" The doctor simply said, "I'm sorry", and left the room. There were many different reactions and emotions from the family. Some ran from the room crying and collapsed in the hall, some sat silently and cried, others stared in shock, while others said we needed to go pray harder. We all held each other and tried to comfort one another.

After a few minutes, I walked down the hall to your room

and stood there and stared at you. I told the nurses not to turn any of the machines off. I then looked at you as I had many other times in the past 21 hours and said, "Kevin, you get back here! You have a purpose to live out! Tell Jesus you can't stay!" I was as determined as I had been from the moment I heard about the wreck that you were going to come out of this. I kept saying, "All is well with Kevin." I knew God was no respecter of persons and if he could do it once, He could do it again for me.

I remembered the story of the Shunammite women who didn't give up on her son. She continued to say, "All is well," and God raised him from the dead. (See 2 Kings 4:8-37.) I wanted so much to pick you up to hold and rock you. You are my baby boy. Your whole life was like a video playing in my head. I told God, "This isn't enough. I want more time. He's supposed to make a difference in this world." Little did I know how true that would be, just not in the ways that I thought you would.

WHEN TO SAY WHEN

Minutes turned into hours, and through the rest of the morning and into the afternoon family and friends were all in and out of your room. There were people praying for you in the hospital, the city, and around the world, thanks to social media. It was comforting to know we had so many praying with us for you.

There was such a battle going on inside of me. I was not ready to let you go, but really who is ever ready to let someone they love go, especially your child. I needed to sit and collect my thoughts. When I left your room, I didn't want to be too far so the hospital staff allowed us to use the small room just outside the TICU doors. I went in there to sit and rest for a few minutes and started to cry. There were several people in the room; I looked at my friend Lori and said, "When do you know when to say when?" She answered, "I can't tell you when that is. Only you will know." I knew at that moment that it was up to you, it was your choice. There was nothing more I could do. It was about 4:00 pm when I went back to your room. I walked over to my usual spot on the left side of your bed. Instead of talking to you out loud this time I leaned down and whispered in your right ear. "Kev, mom's not ready for you to go." And I heard your voice as well as I could hear my own say, "Mom, it's too painful." I stood up and looked at you thinking I really heard you out loud, but I didn't. I know that God knew I would not give up unless I knew without a doubt you didn't want to come back. I believe Jesus said to you, "Dude, your mom is banging on the gates of Heaven and if you don't let her know you don't want to go back, I will have to send you back." I think He showed you how life would be if you came back, the rehabilitation, the recovery, and maybe even a lesser quality of life because of the extent of your injuries. Then He showed you the lives that would be impacted and saved if you stayed with Him, because He knew your Momma would use this horrible tragedy to impact the world for the better.

How little did I know the life ahead, a life without you physically here. As hard as it was to accept I knew you made the better choice. You were in the face of Jesus! How selfish of me to try and make you come back to this cold, ugly, mean world that forced you to leave too soon. So I looked at you, took a deep breath and said, "Ok Kev, Mom will be okay. I love you! I will let you go." At that moment, I felt a part of me die inside. My heart shattered and was bleeding, there was a huge gaping hole, and the pain was one that is unimaginable and cannot be described in words. It was time to say goodbye.

My sweet boy, you brought so much joy and laughter to my life, as well as everyone who ever met you. There will be forever a void in so many lives that only you could fill. Now we are left with memories and wishing there was time to make many more. Please tell Jesus to come quickly, because I don't know how to live in a world without you in it. You were supposed to be here for me to watch you get married to the love of your life, have babies and be an amazing father, have a career, continue to bring fun and laughter to everyone, and visit me when I'm old. How do I do this, how do I say goodbye? Goodbye sounds so final. So instead I will say, "I'll see you soon!" because I know this is not the end. I know you are in my future waiting for me!

Until then, I will make sure you live on in the hearts of everyone by telling your story! I will make sure you get justice for this wrong done to you! I'll love you forever my sweet boy, my Sunshine! See you soon!

Love,
Momma

HOW DO I SAY GOODBYE

CHOICES

Chapter 2

THE NEXT SEVEN

STEPPING INTO A DIFFERENT REALITY-Monday, AUGUST 1, 2011

DURING OUR TIME of being told Kevin was brain dead and the hours that followed, my Daddy's doctor said he had a symptom of something contagious and needed to quarantine him. And since his wife, Bobby, was exposed to it she would be staying with him. Daddy had, however, improved enough to be moved to the step-down ICU floor and would be quarantined there. I personally think the doctor did this so my Daddy wouldn't overhear what had happened to Kevin. We would then be able to plan Kevin's service and have the funeral, and not feel like we had to be there for Daddy too. Because of the severity of the wreck, it was all over the news for days, so they couldn't even have the TV on in his room. They went to great measures to ensure Daddy did not hear what had happened.

All that was left to do after making the decisions regarding organ donation was to go home. Home, where Kevin lived and would NEVER EVER come again. As we were leaving the ICU area the nurse handed me a bag. I opened the bag and the smell of blood was so strong! In it was Kevin's Buffalo Wild Wings uniform that had been cut off him and just one size 15 shoe. I asked about the other shoe and she said if it's not there he didn't come in with it. I couldn't figure out what could have happened that he was only wearing one shoe. I would later find out.

I had envisioned leaving the hospital much differently. I thought I would be leaving with Kevin, planning a rotation of family members to help with his recovery and rehabilitation, rearranging furniture to accommodate a hospital bed and so on. I never in a million years would have thought I would be leaving WITHOUT Kevin, carrying a white plastic bag with his bloody clothes, and going to plan a funeral.

At about 6:45 pm, my husband, Tom, and oldest son, Derek, went downstairs to the ICU Waiting Room to collect and pack our things. We were embraced by friends who had stayed to pray for us during the decisions about organ donation. Strangers who had been waiting on news of their own loved one or waiting for the next visitation time were coming over and giving their condolences. Some of them had been there before we arrived with Daddy and some had come during the past 5 days. You could see in their eyes that they were either thankful that their loved one was improving or hoping they did not have to start on this journey of loss.

GOING HOME WITHOUT KEVIN

After gathering our things and loading everything into the car we started on the 18-minute drive toward home. We were quiet, not really knowing what to say or how to truly articulate how we were feeling. I don't really remember what was even said. The only thing I remember was going through my phone. I had been taking pictures and videos of Daddy's progress. I thought I would do the same with Kevin. I don't remember how many I had, but when I looked through them I started screaming and gave my phone to Derek and told him to delete them. (This was my first lesson in not making hasty decisions when you are grieving. It may sound strange to you that later I would rather have the pictures. But you will understand later.) Derek asked me if I was sure I wanted to delete them. I assured him I never wanted to see them again.

The drive normally didn't feel so long but this day it felt like it took hours. We finally made it home and as we pulled in the driveway I sat there staring at the house. All at once a flood of memories hit me in the face like a brick. This house was where I brought Kevin home from the hospital when he was born. This house was where Kevin played in the yard getting dirty, playing ball, riding big wheels, bicycles, go-carts and 4wheelers, playing ninja turtles and power rangers, sparring with homemade light sabers, decorated Christmas trees, unwrapped countless presents, and the list kept going. This house was where Kevin grew up over the years. This is where all his belongings were. Derek collected our things from the car and headed toward the house while Tom helped me out of the car. We didn't get halfway up the sidewalk before it happened. I collapsed, screaming and crying uncontrollably. Derek dropped everything and ran to help Tom hold me up. They carried me over to the swing in the yard and held me and cried with me. I kept saying, "I cannot walk in the house without my baby!" It was so hard to breathe. I thought I would die right there. I didn't want to live another day. This was uncharted territory. I thought to myself, "This is the worst thing that has ever happened to me and my family. How will we ever survive this?!"

I don't know how long we were out in the front yard on the swing, but it was a while before I could get to the porch. I stood at the door, took a deep breath and made my first step in my front door. As I came in everything looked different, the colors were muted and dull. I was seeing everything through the lens of grief. I felt like I was in a thick fog. Little did I know that the foggy feeling would last for years to come. That evening there were a few people who came by to bring food that I couldn't bring myself to eat. At this point I had not eaten in six days since I heard about my Daddy. I just wanted to go to sleep and wake up to life rewound. When I finally did lay down, I cried uncontrollably as Tom held me. I cried myself to sleep, but there wasn't much sleep for me that night. I dreamed over and over about Kevin's wreck. I would either be in the van with Kevin or standing on the side of the road screaming for him to get out of the way, and then, CRASH! This would jolt me awake and I hoped that I wouldn't dream about the crash again. (But I did dream the crash over and over every night for the next year and a half.)

EXHAUSTED AND OVERWHELMED

Tuesday, August 2, 2011, I woke up completely exhausted, drained, and realizing that yesterday was, in fact, reality. Tom and Derek had already been up for a while. I came downstairs to the kitchen to get some coffee, hoping I could drink it and keep it down. I knew at some point I would have to eat to be able to have the physical strength to face the next few days. I was so overwhelmed with all that I knew had to be done. But we couldn't plan any date for viewing or the funeral until the organ recovery surgery was complete and then Kevin would be sent to have an autopsy before he could go to the funeral home to be cleaned up, prepared and dressed for the funeral. With all of this going through my head, the phone rang. It was the investigator working the wreck. He asked if he could come by for a few minutes. He had some paperwork he needed me to sign. I figured the sooner he came the sooner charges could be filed. Even though Tom and I had worked in prison ministry with inmates for almost ten years, there were still a lot of details about the process we were not aware of. I will talk about that later. Two officers showed up at my house about twenty minutes later. One of them did all the talking while the other stood silently. The officer asked a couple of questions. "Did Kevin have a wife or kids?" "Where was Kevin coming from the night of the wreck?" "Did he drink?" He had a paper for me to sign giving consent to check Kevin's blood to prove he was not drinking. I assured him that Kevin did not drink and signed the paper and told him to test away! This officer did NOT get on my good side from the start and with what we were going through, he just added to the frustration. Every question I asked him, his answer was, "I can't discuss that with you." This seemed to be his answer for everything. I realized that we weren't getting anywhere with the conversation and as nicely as I could I sent them on their way. That frustration would be for another day. I wasn't going to deal with them any longer. I had a funeral to plan.

PLANNING MY BABY'S FUNERAL

We started planning things that we could. It wasn't long before my Mom and Stepa arrived and we started going through pictures for the video montage and 4'x 5' picture board. We went through his clothes and chose Kevin's last outfit. There was no question that he would wear Batman as he always did. From the time he was four years old he loved Batman. We decided he would wear his favorite fedora hat to cover the top right side of the front of his head where it had to be shaved to insert the device the nurses called a "bolt" that was used to monitor Kevin's brain pressure. We carefully bagged all the items to be ready to take to the funeral home. We called Wilson's Funeral Home and made an appointment for the next day to discuss what we wanted to do. We started going through Kevin's things when I realized there wasn't much to go through. You see, growing up Kevin was giving his things away all the time. I would be so upset because we didn't have a lot of money, but Kevin and his brother, Derek, always had what they needed and we did what we could to afford the extras. It didn't matter to Kevin that he gave his things away. He was just a giver and was so sweet and generous. That was a habit he continued into adulthood. There wasn't much to go through because he gave his things away. He would know that someone needed something he had and give it to them and go without and never complain. All of his personal belongings fit in a 10'x10' bedroom. I decided what I wanted to keep for myself and put the items in a little black foot locker of Kevin's. (To this day I open it to reminisce and I can still smell him).

It was now the mid-afternoon; more people brought food, and family and friends were coming by. Among them were my BFFs, which we lovingly called our little group "The 6Pack", (no alcohol involved LOL). We always knew how to be there for each other. We had been here before almost seven years ago when my friend, Cathy's son died suddenly a month before his

21st birthday. We had rallied around her then and now they were there for me. We were all in Kevin's little room along with my Mom. We were showing them some of Kevin's items we were going to display at his funeral. And we got off on telling stories about funny things he did. All of our kids had grown up together, attended youth group together, and had sleepovers. Everyone had stories to share. All at once my friend Gina spoke up and said, "You may think I'm crazy, but I have to tell you something." Here is what Gina had to tell me in her own words.

> "The morning started with a heavy heart at the thought of such a young life, taken, way too soon. I decided to pray for peace for the entire family and all of the heartbroken friends mourning the loss of Kevin. I went into the breakfast nook, sat at the table and entered into prayer. While praying, I started to cry. I crossed my arms on the table, and just laid my head down. I had held back my tears in order to be strong for Tiki and the family, but in my private place, the tears came and came. Through the tears, I prayed, then suddenly, I felt a presence that made me open my eyes and look around the room, but no one was there. I laid my head back down on the table, and reentered prayer. Within minutes, I felt the same presence.
>
> Now, usually, anything like that makes me want to get up and run from the room. However, this wasn't the case. I felt a peace that made me stop crying. I heard a small whisper in my ear. It said, "Tell my mom I made it and it's amazing. I didn't know it would be like this." I raised my head up, looked around the room, then thought to myself, that I must be delusional or just overwhelmed with emotion. So I ignored the voice or what I thought was a voice. I continued praying, still very emotional, and again I heard the voice say,

"Tell my mom it's amazing." I thought to myself, I'm not going to tell her that, she'll think I'm crazy, or just making up something to try to make her feel better. I pushed the words that were said out of my mind, and continued praying. Once again, the voice said, "Tell my mom". As I continued to question if I was really hearing what I thought I was hearing, the voice continued, very sweetly, but very persistently, "Tell my mom I made it and it's amazing. I didn't know it would be like this."

I finally realized this was really happening, and said out loud, "Ok! Fine. I'll tell her, but what if she doesn't believe me. (I had a hard time believing it myself.) I'll tell her anyway." The sweet presence, which I now know was Kevin, remained in the room, as if he was letting me know how happy he was that he finally got his message through to me. It brought a warmth and calmness to my heart. I just sat there, looking out the window with the biggest smile on my face. I couldn't believe Kevin actually blessed me with such a special request. I've heard of this happening to people, but never thought it would happen to me. I had thoughts of what I would say, how would I tell you. I hoped you wouldn't think I'm nuts. It didn't matter. I didn't know how, when, or where to tell you, but I knew I had to do it as soon as possible. Kevin loves you with all of his heart."

When she said, "It's AMAZING", my Mom and I started crying. That was Kevin's word! AMAZING! I knew Kevin had sent me a message and to make it even sweeter was to have one of my best friends deliver it! This was a light shining in my dark fog. This has helped me through many tough days since.

Afterward we went on with more planning, phone calls, going through pictures, and listening to songs, trying to choose the perfect ones. Derek suggested to have all Kevin's favorite theme music play on a loop during the viewing, like Batman, Ninja Turtles, Power Rangers, all different video games, and more. I thought it was a great idea, so Derek found all the music and put the CD together. One of Derek and Kevin's friends from youth group back in the day, Michael Ketterer, had a new album out for a few weeks. I had downloaded it when it was released and there were a couple of songs that I really liked that I had no idea would be used a few weeks later for Kevin's funeral. We picked a third song that was one of Kevin's favorites, "Your Guardian Angel" by Red Jumpsuit Apparatus. You will hear more about how special this song is later.

We decided to throw a party the way Kevin would have. We wanted people who came to be able to browse through all the displays and know who Kevin was by the time they left. We asked everyone to wear Batman or their favorite super hero, or video game t-shirts. We thought about how much Kevin and his friends enjoyed playing video games and the fact that he was going to open his own gaming cafe for kids to come and have a safe place to play and have fun. So we decided to setup a gaming station for his friends to play in memory of Kevin. We took his huge posters of video games and comics, his bowling bag, ball, shoes (size 15!) and winning awards, his letterman high school jackets, and Ninja Turtles. Buffalo Wild Wings gave us several items to display, and video game stores donated displays of his favorite games to display. We pretty much emptied Kevin's room to put it all on display. There were hundreds of pictures between the looping video that Derek had put together and the framed photos. After all our "Kevin party" planning we got the call around 8:30 p.m. that he was being taken to surgery to become a superhero. I knew the call would come but when it did, it was just another moment in time that felt so final.

SURROUNDED BY CASKETS AND GRAVES

Wednesday, August 3, 2011, I woke up knowing that it was going to be a very long, hard day. Kevin's surgery had just been completed, and he was transferred to the medical examiner's office for autopsy. I wondered how Kevin's recipients were doing and what kind of day they would experience with their new gift of life. But there was no time to ponder on that because we had a morning appointment to go to Wilson's Funeral Home to make arrangements. My BFF, Christy, met us there. She played a HUGE part in helping us plan and think of things that I just couldn't think of because of the fog of grief I was walking around in. The first thing we did was walk through a large room full of caskets to choose the perfect one. I thought to myself, "How do I pick the right casket for my baby? Nothing about this is right!" I felt like crawling in one myself and just dying. All I could do was cry. It was as if a water pipe had cracked and the leak couldn't be fixed. We finally picked a black one and decided to decorate it in a Batman theme. Afterwards we went into another room and filled out all the paperwork. We chose to have the viewing and service at the church we attended at the time. We asked the funeral staff to also wear superheroes (and they did!). We knew Kevin would want to go out in style. We had tried to get the Batman car to come and lead the procession, but it was booked. We didn't want Kevin to have his last ride in a hearse, so we chose the glass enclosed carrier to be pulled by a motorcycle. Okay, I know that sounds a little bit "out there", but Kevin loved motorcycles and wanted one. My Daddy was still in the hospital and still didn't know about what had happened. This was a way that my Daddy's riding buddies could be there for him since he couldn't.

Derek had created a keepsake pamphlet for everyone to take at the sign-in book, as well as the video montage, so we didn't have to choose any of those items. We were finally finished with the first stop of the day. As we were leaving, I took a closer look at something on a display table that had caught my eye from across the room as we were sitting at the table filling out paperwork. To my surprise it was a necklace with a fingerprint charm! I ask the man we had worked with how to get one of those. And he told me that it was something I would need to order at that time to be able to get Kevin's finger print. It would then be on file for any more jewelry pieces we would want in the future. Of course, I had to have one!

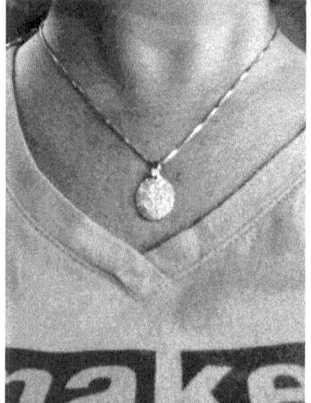

Now we were on to our next stop across town to another funeral home to choose a place to bury Kevin. We arrived and were greeted by one of the sweetest men. He was the person who would be working with us. I was very glad, because he made us feel at ease and was attentive to what we needed and wanted. He took us to the plots that were available and fit what we wanted. We walked through the cemetery around all the other graves, again finding myself looking for the perfect place to bury my baby. We chose the one that was closest to where my BFF's son was buried. Afterwards, we went back to the office to fill out more paperwork. I had not even really thought about a headstone or what we would want it to look like. When we were asked the question, I was just overwhelmed and the cracked, leaky pipe cracked even more. I thought to myself, "How much more of this can I do? This is all too much! But I have to make everything perfect for my baby. God, please help me!! I can't do this without You!" The nice man then said we could wait to make that decision if I needed to. But I knew I needed to do it now and get this part behind me. Again, we didn't go with the standard headstone. It had to stand out, just like Kevin did. We chose a beautiful bronze colored one with a customized image that his brother, Derek, designed.

(It would not be until Kevin's birthday eight months later when it was finished and finally installed).

Our last stop was to shop for our Batman t-shirts. I personally had not ever had a Batman t-shirt. Kevin would have thought it was so cool for his mom to wear Batman. I wish I had thought enough to do something so simple for him when he could have enjoyed it. I waited too late. Now I'm buying one to wear to his Life Celebration Party. Derek, Tom, and I went to several stores and bought t-shirts, wristbands, and several other Batman items. We were finally done except for a couple of things that could be done the next day. I was so glad for that process to be over. Unless you have been in a traumatic situation like this, you cannot begin to understand all the things that feel like a brick in the face. I was glad that there were no more bricks today.

HEARING ALL THE NOISE

Thursday, August 4, 2011, Today would be less stressful with little to do other than take all Kevin's things to the church to setup for display later in the day. I was glad to have some time to try and breathe. But less activity only created more anxiety. There was more time to think and there was a major battle going on in my mind. Not that it had not been there in my mind since before Kevin was pronounced brain dead, but there had been little time to pay attention to the war going on in my head. There had been so much to do and plan. But now I was hearing all the noise. I had to remind myself over and over that I chose to forgive! At the time I couldn't find the words to pray. I just continually cried and said, "God, I don't understand, but I trust You to bring good from this horrible tragedy."

CHOICES

PLEASE DON'T MAKE ME OPEN MY EYES

Friday, August 5, 2011, I woke up this morning and didn't want to open my eyes. I wanted today to be the day I woke up to find everything from the past 10 days had been a terrible dream. But the longer I lay there the more I knew that keeping my eyes closed would not change the fact that today there would be people from everywhere coming to say goodbye to my Kev. I had hoped that the funeral home was able to fix him enough to have an open casket. I wanted to go and see for myself. His hair had to be just right. So I asked my mom to go with me. The funeral home said they would be ready for us to come at 2:30pm. This would give us time to make sure and approve any changes that might need to be made or decide to have a closed casket.

Mom and I left and had a few errands to do before going to the funeral home. The only thing I remember was we went to a little clothing store and there was a smiley face watch and mom bought it for me to remind me of Kevin's smile. His nickname was Sunshine because he smiled and brought fun and laughter to everyone. Mom was right. Every time I looked at it I would smile through the tears. And I had no idea how many times I would need a reminder over the next few hours, days, months, and even years.

FIXING KEVIN'S HAIR

When we arrived at the funeral home our funeral director gave us instructions and tried to prepare us for what we were about to see. We had some idea because Mom and I had the privilege of doing her mom, my Nanny's, hair and makeup one last time for her homegoing service three years before. But nothing could really prepare someone to see their child. The director led us through a door that was labeled "Staff Only." We walked through what looked like a breakroom to another door opening, and there he was. Kevin's lifeless body was lying on a stainless steel heavy duty table. He was dressed in the outfit we had chosen. His head was on a small square headrest and his long curling blondish-brown hair was hanging off the end of the table. They had done a wonderful job repairing the long gash that was from his forehead across his left eye and down his cheek. You couldn't even see where it had been.

Mom and I adjusted some of the coloring on Kevin's face and I fixied his hair so it would be just right for all his family and friends to see him one last time. As Mom and I worked with Kevin we talked to him as if he were listening. As we talked to him the tears flowed and I thought to myself, "I can't believe this is really happening." I was fixing Kevin's hair as I had done his whole life. Most every hair cut he ever got was from me. Every wild and crazy thing he wanted to do to his hair I did except dying it black! (That, he let someone else do! That was a whole other story that I won't go into, but it took months of coloring to get it back to normal). As upset as I was over the black hair, it was still a memory and that was all I had left. I thought about the fact that he was growing it out to donate it to children with hair loss and now he couldn't because it wasn't long enough. Memory after memory played in my head and I just kept feeling his hair knowing it would be the last time. Some may think what Mom and I did for Kevin that day to be gross or morbid and crazy as it sounds it was a precious and private last few minutes to spend with him where he wasn't hooked to all kinds of machines and he was dressed as he always was. It was as if he was sleeping and peaceful. I had people try and talk me out of going, but I'm glad I didn't listen. It was a sweet moment that Mom and I got to share with Kevin one last time.

THE VIEWING – ('PRE-PARTY')

The family and close friends gathered at 4:30 p.m. to go in and have time with Kevin before everyone started coming at 5:00 p.m. When the people started coming in, it was overwhelming to see the number of people. There were thousands and the line was across the auditorium and out to the door for hours. Derek, Tom, and I, along with other family stood beside Kevin's casket and greeted each person with hugs and smiles through the tears. There were caring people who tried to get me to take a break and sit for a while, but this was what I felt I needed to do. I needed to talk with each person. There were many stories told about Kevin I would have missed if I had taken a break. There were people I didn't know who only knew Kevin as a server. He had made such an impression on them that when he changed jobs and moved from IHOP to Buffalo Wild Wings, they followed him. They would go when he was there and if they had to wait it was okay. There were doctors, attorneys, firemen, and people from many other professions and walks of life who came and shared stories of the impact Kevin had made on them. I was amazed that my son, a 25 years old, 6 feet 5 inch, long-haired, gamer, who loved life and lived it to the fullest making people laugh, could have left such an impression on so many. It gave me so much joy to know that Kevin was loved by so many people.

One special moment was when Kevin's co-workers and boss from BWWs came in. One of the girls proceeded to tell me that Kevin had taken the test to be promoted to a Floor Trainer and they had gotten word of the promotion earlier that week and his name badge with his new position had come that day. She handed it to me and I hugged her and the others in the group and told them thank you. I then turned to pin the name badge on Kevin's Batman jacket. He would have been so excited to get that promotion, but he didn't get the chance.

There were so many who came up and said they had never seen the likes of how we displayed all Kevin's things and the video games going on. They said if someone came in and didn't know Kevin, they definitely knew him by the time they left. There were people everywhere sharing fun memories about Kevin. It really was a party like Kevin would have thrown himself. No one wanted to leave, but we finally left late that evening knowing we did Kevin proud. Now to try and get some rest before tomorrow. I prayed and asked God for His strength as I cried myself to sleep.

THE PARTY NO ONE WANTED TO ATTEND

Saturday, August 6, 2011. TODAY. This is the day, the Life Celebration Party that we had been planning for a week, but none of us wanted to go to. Just like the past few days, I managed to put makeup on while crying. I fixed my hair and put on my new Batman t-shirt. Then Derek, Tom, and I left to go to the church. We arrived at 10:00am to meet the rest of the family and have a few minutes together before everyone started coming in for Kevin's Life Celebration Party.

KEVIN'S LIFE CELEBRATION PARTY

People started arriving and before we knew it the church was full. There were even people standing in the back around the walls of the auditorium. It was a sea of Batman along with other superheroes and video game characters everywhere! I thought to myself, "I wish Kevin could see this." I was so proud that my boy had meant so much to so many people. It made me realize how important it is to tell those around you what they mean to you, because you never know when your time to do so is gone. I was glad I had no regrets about that with Kevin. I raised my boys to know how very much I loved them and how special they were to me, and how proud I was to be their Mom. If there is one thing they knew, it was that I love them. As I sat there thinking it warmed my heart to see everyone and know they loved him too.

The service started at 11:00 a.m. Pastor Rich Brock greeted everyone and opened with prayer, Michael Ketterer sang, "Dusty Road," Pastors Alan and Terri Crider read the obituary, Michael sang a second song, "Beautiful." One of Kevin's best friends, Casey Brostek, shared Kevin stories, my BFF, Gina Griffin, shared about Kevin giving her a message for me, Tom and I shared some poems Kevin had written. Derek and Alicia sang, "Your Guardian Angel," and then Dean Sikes founder of YOU Matter gave the message. We had asked Dean to give an altar call at the end of the service. He did and there were 48 people who came to make their lives right with God. It was so special to see. Dean then asked Michael to come and sing "Beautiful" again. The atmosphere was so sweet. Pastor Rich closed the service and gave instruction for the gravesite service.

THE NEXT SEVEN

KEVIN'S LITTLE PIECE OF LAND

As we all left the church and drove to the cemetery there were cars as far as you could see following the motorcycle pulling the glass enclosed carrier with Kevin's casket inside escorted by fifteen motorcycles, in honor of my Daddy who was still in the hospital, taking him on his last ride. There were so many different feelings while making our way down Highway 153, the same road where Kevin worked, the same road where the drunk driver drove on the wrong side of the highway and hit Kevin head on. And now, the same road where he would be buried. Before we arrived at the cemetery, it started raining. I had hoped the rain would hold off, but I think it was welcomed by many to disguise their tears.

What was a short thirty-minute drive felt like forever, but on the other hand I wished I would wake up from this nightmare so it would be over and I wouldn't have to bury my sweet boy. I didn't wake up. We were there. As we were driving a video was filming following behind Kevin. There was a reflection of a Batman on the windshield that looked as if it was moving and following Kevin. I think it was a message from him saying he was with us. When we came to the area of the gravesite, Kevin's friends gathered around along with his Dad, brother Derek, and cousin Dustin and stood in the rain waiting to carry him to his final resting place. They pulled Kevin from the carrier and carried him up the hill to the tent as everyone gathered around to hear the final words. Derek and Alicia sang, "Give Me Jesus", and everyone joined in. Tom's brother, Pastor Tim Finlayson, gave the graveside message. And Pastor Rich Brock led us in one last song before his closing prayer. I just sat there and cried staring at the casket and Kevin's picture. It still all felt like a nightmare. It was hard to focus with the fog in my mind. I thought to myself, *"God, is this really it? How will I get through this? I WANT TO DIE! Just take me now. I don't want to do this! GOD PLEASE HELP ME!!!"*

People were coming up and hugging me and the family. I looked around and there were many of us who didn't want to leave. We watched the cemetery staff lower Kevin into the ground. I stood there at the opening of the deep hole in disbelief at the sight of a black casket with a Batman emblem on the top at the bottom of the hole with Kevin inside. I pulled one of the white roses from his flowers and slowly let it go, and watched it fall on the top of his casket. Then the family members, who wanted to, took a handful of dirt and sprinkled it in on the casket. All Kevin's friends released blue, yellow, and black balloons after we were finished and yelled, "We love you, Kevin!"

There were many family and friends who went to the "After Party" at Buffalo Wild Wings where Kevin had worked. Kevin's co-workers who couldn't attend the service were glad we came.

For them, it was their way of being a part of the day to celebrate him. We ate, told stories about Kevin, and laughed along with the tears. I kept thinking to myself how much Kevin would have loved this day and all we were doing. The party continued to the bowling alley to do an activity that Kevin loved. There were over thirty of us. We had fun for Kevin. I was glad for all the activity that day after the service. It reminded me of Kevin's favorite thing, FUN!

I have included links to the Facebook Album of Kevin's Life Celebration, as well as the Youtube links for the service videos. *(The video was recorded mainly for my Daddy to be able to watch and have some sort of closure after his recovery).*

Sunday, August, 7, 2011, I got up after only a couple hours of sleep as I had done since I left the hospital without my Kevin. It was quiet, there were no plans to be made, no arrands to run, no nothing. For the rest of the world life when back to "normal", but for me my normal had been shattered into too many pieces to count. I just wanted to die instead of feel this pain. It was too intense. But I found the will to do the only thing I knew to do, so I got dressed and went to church to try and find some peace.

Kevin's Celebration Party, August 5-6, 2011
https://www.facebook.com/kevinsunshineyates/media_set?set=a.10150341084593198.352475.541398197&type=3

Video 1 - Pastor Rich Brock opening prayer, Michael Ketterer sings, "Dusty Road"
https://www.youtube.com/watch?v=C1c20KwjPz4

CHOICES

Video 2 - Pastors Alan and Terri Crider reading obituary and sharing
https://www.youtube.com/watch?v=LGaZ5eHcVBA

Video 3 - Michael Ketterer sing, "Beautiful"
https://www.youtube.com/watch?v=P-q_ZUpF0ek

Video 4 - Casey and Gina sharing
https://www.youtube.com/watch?v=IAiFGiHSyVY

Video 5 - Tom and Tiki speaking
https://www.youtube.com/watch?v=WWWiUhigai0

Video 6 - "Your Guardian Angel" Derek and Alicia
https://www.youtube.com/watch?v=LS4qurt0yd8

Video 7 - Dean Sikes message
https://www.youtube.com/watch?v=G_AzmKmA86s

Video 8 - Dean Sikes closing
https://www.youtube.com/watch?v=0bsViJVqBWc

Video 9 - Michael Ketterer sings "Beautiful" again
https://www.youtube.com/watch?v=KMAURhk-ins

Video 10 - Procession to grave-site
https://www.youtube.com/watch?v=YgMN24b80Ng

Video 11 - Derek and Alicia sing, "Give Me Jesus"
https://www.youtube.com/watch?v=o5eDzbuDPc8

Video 12 - Pastor Tim Finlayson graveside message
https://www.youtube.com/watch?v=DSjQ1iL_lMo

Video 13 - Pastor Rich Brock closing and balloon release
https://www.youtube.com/watch?v=M41ERzYdln0

Chapter 3

A LIFE FOR A LIFE

ONE OF THE HARDEST DECISIONS of my life was saying "Yes" to Kevin being an organ donor. However, I knew it was what Kevin would have wanted. He was the kindest, most compassionate, and giving person. He was a very simple man and didn't have many possessions. If Kevin knew someone needed something, and he had it, he would give it away, do without, and never think twice about it.

One conversation that solidified my decision was a couple of years prior to Kevin's wreck. He and I were talking about organ donation after one of his friends, Blake, (age 17), collapsed suddenly at work and later died. Blake was an organ donor and Kevin thought of him as a "Super Hero" because Blake saved lives. Kevin told me, "Mom, if something ever happens to me I want to be an organ donor and save lives. I want to be a Super Hero like Blake."

Well, of course he wanted to be a Super Hero! He called himself Batman. As I said earlier, he loved Batman from the time he was about four years old. I told Kevin how proud I was of him for making such a selfless decision. It was just a few minutes of conversation then we went on to talk about other things while I was cooking dinner. Not once did I ever think that I would have to be the one to make that decision for him and choose what to donate.

It was now 4:30 p.m. on August 1, 2011, and the next two hours were grueling and heart wrenching, spent with family members and the Tennessee Donor Services Representative going through the list of what Kevin would donate, and signing paperwork for his organs and tissues that would save or improve someone else's life. As we finished, I asked the donor services representative about the communication process. When and how I could contact the recipients? I knew I wanted to meet the recipients as soon as I could. However, I was informed that I needed to wait at least a year and the meeting had to be mutual consent between the donor family and recipient. I just prayed that the recipients would want to meet Kevin's family. To see them living life would allow us to find a little joy from this horrible and senseless tragedy.

We were told that we could wait with Kevin while they finished with all the testing and matching of recipients. They said someone would call us when it was time for the recovery surgery--that it could take several hours before it was time, or we could go home and try to get some rest. There were so many things to be done and plans to be made for Kevin's Celebration of Life. The list was overwhelming! So I chose to go home. I had already said, my "See you later." There were other family members who chose to stay with Kevin and walk with him on the evening of August 2, 2011, as he was rolled to the elevator and said their goodbyes. They waited until his recovery surgery was complete on the morning of August 3, 2011, before going home.

RECIPIENTS

Kevin saved four lives with his organs and improved the lives of many more with his tissues.

Kevin's LIVER gave a second chance at life for a 72 year old gentleman. He had been on the transplant list since September 2004. He was married, and had two children, and was retired. This gentleman unfortunately passed away six months after his transplant due to an unrelated heart attack. My thoughts and prayers are with his family and I hope someday to at least get to talk with them and find out who he was.

Kevin's RIGHT KIDNEY gave life to a 48 year old gentleman. He had been on the transplant list since April 2004. He had never been married, and had no children. He has a mother and two younger sisters and several nieces and nephews. He volunteers for the kidney foundation. He enjoys playing the guitar and spending time with his family.

Kevin's LEFT KIDNEY and PANCREAS gave new life to a 49 year old lady. She had been on the transplant list since September 2010. She was separated from her husband, with one child. We were given no other information about her.

Kevin's HEART gave life to a 48 year old gentleman. He had been on the transplant list since May 2011. He had been married 17 years and had 3 children. He is also a minister.

Kevin's donation of skin, dermal skin, heart valves and associated blood vessels, pericardium, blood vessels of the abdomen and legs, bone and connective tissue of the hips, legs and ankles might have been utilized by many individuals needing reconstructive surgeries, due to trauma or disease, and may help to improve their quality of life.

Kevin's eyes were too damaged to be donated. We were not able to donate Kevin's lungs due to them being lacerated. Both were a result of all the glass on the left side of his van shattering during the impact in the wreck.

We received a couple of letters with updates on the progress of the recipients. I prayed for them and their recovery. I so wanted to meet them and couldn't wait for the time to come when I could send them letters. This was also a drawn out process of me sending my letter to the donor services office. They forwarded my letter to the transplant center and then they sent it to the recipient only IF the recipient agreed to receive communication from their donor's family. If they chose to write, the process was reversed for me to receive their letter. In our letters we could only write basic information with no last names or contact information. We were then given forms to sign that our information could be released. If we chose to meet, it would be coordinated at a later time.

You may start thinking, what does this part have to do with organ donation? But bear with me; I must share some background to lead you to where we are going.

A BIRTHDAY CELEBRATION

APRIL 2, 2012. This day was a very bittersweet day. We had been working for months with Derek and Alicia on recording "Your Guardian Angel" and making a video tribute to Kevin to be released on this day. It was so exciting!

A LIFE FOR A LIFE

We had been posting on social media, Derek and Alicia were interviewed on the news channels prior to this day and there was quite a buzz about it. We were up that morning posting and emailing to announce the release. However, it was also a sad day. It was Kevin's 26th birthday, the first of many we would celebrate without him. Here is the link to "Your Gaurdian Angel. I hope you enjoy watching it. *https://youtu.be/hzAe3CcKKIY*

After our morning of promoting the song and video to start the celebration of Kevin, we went to our local IHOP (where Kevin had worked before Buffalo Wild Wings). Kevin still had many friends there and we enjoyed seeing them and they always had a story to share about Kevin. We had a wonderful breakfast, then it was time to head back home. We had lots of other plans for the day and more promoting to do for the song and video. After we arrived back home, Tom, Derek, and I were all at the kitchen table with our laptops posting and promoting away. There was a call from one of the news stations wanting an interview about the release of the song. So off we were again to interview. This was an unscheduled part of the eventful day, but it was important and it would help get the word out. When we came back home, we collected the mail from the mailbox and went in the house to continue promoting and laid the mail on the table.

After a few minutes went by I started flipping through the mail and saw an envelope from Tennessee Donor Services. I had received several letters in the past with basic information about Kevin's recipients and letters just to encourage me. They were always so thoughtful. And I thought what a nice gesture to send something on Kevin's birthday. I opened the envelope and could hardly believe my eyes. It was a letter from Kevin's heart recipient!!!!! I gasped and clutched the letter to my chest and started laughing, crying, and jumping up and down! Tom and Derek were asking what it was and it was a few minutes before I could speak so they could understand me. When I finally composed myself I sat down to read the letter aloud. We all three sat there and cried tears of joy to hear from a little piece of Kevin on his birthday living in a wonderful man named Melvin! There was no better gift for our family that day.

Later that day we went to the cemetery to Kevin's little piece of land to release balloons for Kevin. With family and friends, we stood around his grave with our balloons and handwritten messages for Kevin on them.. One by one we shared stories about Kevin. Some made us cry, but most made us laugh because that was what Kevin was about, making people laugh and have fun. Just before releasing our balloons I told everyone that there was one more person who wanted to share something. I pulled out Melvin's letter and said, "It's from Kevin's heart recipient." Everyone gasped, cheered and clapped, then got very quiet to hear me read the letter. It was a sweet moment and was as if Kevin had come down to give us all one of his famous "tall hugs"!

The next day I immediately contacted Tennessee Donor Services (TDS) to find out the guidelines for writing back to Melvin. When I got off the phone, I went through Kevin's photos to decide which ones I wanted to send with my letter and made copies of them. Then I sat down and started writing. I told Melvin everything I could within the guidelines. After finishing I placed the photos inside, choosing one of Kevin in his fedora hat to be on top. I sealed it all in an envelope and mailed it to

TDS who would forward it to the transplant center and they would send my letter to Melvin. And all that was left to do was WAIT. The waiting was almost tormenting. I have never been so anxious for the mail to run in all my life! Then one day the phone rang and it was Robin, my contact person from TDS. She had Melvin's home phone number for me! I was so nervous! How would I introduce myself? What would I say? What if I get his voicemail? Do I leave a message or try calling back later? The questions just flooded my mind. I slowly dialed the number and it started ringing. When it picked up I thought my heart would stop, and then I heard the voicemail. I left a brief message and my phone number and hung up. Within the hour my phone rang and it was Melvin! His voice was music to my ears. We talked for quite a while and got to know each other. We talked about making plans to meet. Before hanging up we planned a time to talk again to confirm dates for our meeting and then said our goodbyes. I was so happy that I couldn't quit smiling all day.

HEARING THE SOUND OF HIS HEART

SATURDAY, JULY 7, 2012. Finally the day came to meet Melvin! Eight of our family, in two vehicles, headed out early from Chattanooga, Tennessee, to Melvin's home town of Batesville, Mississippi, just forty-five minutes south of Memphis, Tennessee, where Melvin lives. We had chosen his hometown because most of Melvin's family live there and Melvin pastors a church there as well.

The ride felt like it took much longer than six hours. We were all so excited to meet the man carrying Kevin's heart. We arrived at our hotel and checked-in and freshened up before heading back to the lobby to wait for Melvin to arrive. We got the cameras ready to capture the moment and anxiously waited. We had planned to meet at 5:30 p.m. and the clock felt as if it moved slower and slower as each minute went by. And then a maroon truck pulled in the parking lot. It was him! We all lined up to greet him. The door opened and in walked Melvin with his wife Rosemary, and mother, Earlene. He had a big smile on his face. I couldn't wait any longer and ran into his arms! I cried and cried; it was a very bittersweet moment. There were so many emotions that there are not adequate words to describe the moment! I finally let everyone else have a turn to hug Melvin's neck and I hugged Rosemary and Earlene. Everyone was crying and smiling all at the same time.

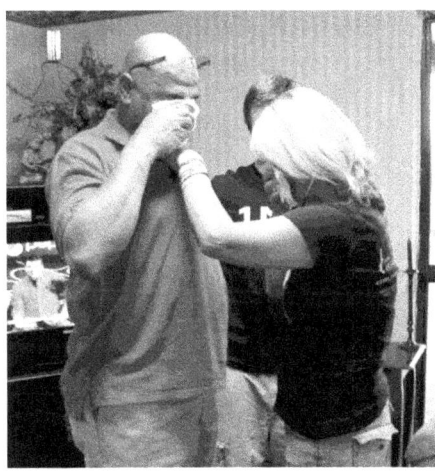

Then came the moment I had been waiting for. Melvin let us listen to Kevin's heart beat with a stethoscope! As I stood there listening to my baby's heart inside this wonderful man's chest my heart swelled with pride. I don't think I have ever been prouder of Kevin than at that moment. He was truly a SUPER HERO!

He had given life to this man whom he had never met or ever heard of, who was so close to death's door when Melvin received Kevin's gift of life. And here he stood in front of me, standing tall, strong and healthy! I just listened to each beat. His heart was beating so strong. I was close to a little piece of Kevin! It was such a special moment that I didn't want it to end. But I had to give my family a turn to listen if they wanted to, so I passed the stethoscope off to Derek. After those who wanted to listen had done so, we talked for a few minutes and then we all left to go to a restaurant just down the street where more of Melvin's family were waiting to have dinner with us. Of course I hopped in the truck with Melvin. I was going to savor every moment I could.

All together there were twenty-one of us. We told stories about Kevin and they told stories about Melvin. We laughed and cried together and bonded as one big family. We didn't want our time to end, but the restaurant was closing so we said our goodbyes until the next day.

FINYATELLISONS

SUNDAY, JULY 8, 2012. We got up Sunday morning and headed to Pilgrim's Rest Baptist Church where Melvin is the pastor. We were going to get to watch him preach! To our surprise when we walk into the church everyone was wearing t-shirts that they had specially made. They were black with a yellow Batman with a heart inside on the front left chest. On the back was a huge Batman logo with a heart on it and Kevin's name, and around the Batman read "OUR HERO SUNSHINE"!

It was a wonderful service. The choir sang beautifully. Melvin presented me with one of the t-shirts and asked me to say a few words. Derek, Mom, and I sang a song for them and Melvin preached. He was so full of life and very animated in his preaching! It warmed my heart to watch him in action knowing that less than a year before he would stand in his pulpit wearing oxygen to preach and could not walk but a few feet before being exhausted because his heart was so sick. Now he had a twenty-five year old heart and there was no stopping him!

After the service the church members put on a spread! There was so much good southern home-cooked food and the fried fish, oh my goodness! It was so good! There were people everywhere. We had so much fun and laughed so hard our faces hurt. It was one big family. We decided to make a new last name for our new family by joining all our names together. We are now the *"Finyatellisons"*.

The time came when we had to head back home to

Chattanooga. I just hugged on Melvin and didn't want to let go, but this wasn't goodbye, we were family now and made a decision to visit as often as we could. And we have done just that.

Since then Melvin and some of his family have come each year on the anniversary date of Kevin moving to Heaven to attend our annual international event we do with our nonprofit, 1N3, to bring awareness of the impact of drunk driving. We have spoken together at a few Tennessee Donor Services events and did a commercial to promote organ donation. We see each other a couple of times of year due to the distance, we talk and text, and keep up with each other on Facebook. I'm so thankful to have a relationship with Melvin and his wonderful family which is now mine too.

MELVIN'S LETTER

I knew this chapter wouldn't be complete without Melvin having a part. I asked him to write whatever he wanted to share and here it is in his words.

"Melvin Ellis is my name and this is a portion of my story which involves my illness, heart transplant, and meeting the Finlayson and Yates families.

In the spring of 2008, I started to become short of breath and short winded. During the early part of 2009, I was at work one night and I thought I was having a heart attack. I was having all the symptoms: sweating, shortness of breath, dizziness, chest pain, and vomiting. I called my wife to come and take me to the hospital. On arrival at the hospital I told the emergency room staff about the symptoms I was having. I was admitted and the staff started running heart tests to see if I did have a heart attack. Some hours later the doctor came back into my room and told me that I didn't have a heart attack, but there was something abnormal showing up on my EKG report that they didn't know what it was; they wanted me to see a heart specialist. I was transported from Delta Medical Hospital to St. Francis Hospital and admitted to the Heart and Cardiac Unit.

After about seven days of testing, they came back and told me that I had a heart disease known as Cardiomyopathy Dilated. It is a disease that affects your heart muscle, usually starting in your main pumping chamber (left ventricle). The ventricles stretches and thins, and can't pump blood freely. I was referred to a local cardiologist. He began to try a series of high dose heart medicines to see if they would strengthen the muscle back around my heart. After months of trying, they saw that the medicine wasn't working.

In June 2009, they decided that I would need a pacemaker, but what I received was a three-in-one which is called a Triventricula Pacemaker, because my heart infractions had dropped below normal. Normal is about 50 and I was at 21 infractions.

From June 2009 through 2010, everything was working fine, but around October or November my heart infractions started dropping at a rapid pace. They had fallen to 12 infractions and that's when they started talking to me about having a heart transplant and becoming a transplant candidate.

My doctor in Memphis, Tennessee, referred me to a heart specialist in Nashville at Vanderbilt Medical Center for testing, x-rays and counseling to become a transplant candidate. In March 2011, I was put on another medicine for congestive heart failure. The medicine was designed to help keep the blood pressure down and help the blood flow through the heart.

In May 2011, I got a virus and it made my heart infractions drop below double digits. I was moved from the non-critical to the critical 1-A list.

In July 2011, I got sick again and my infractions were down to seven. I was scheduled for surgery to receive a mechanical heart on August 5, 2011. However, on August 2, 2011, at 3:30 p.m., I received the call of my life, letting me know that they had found a heart that matched my blood type and the other requirements. We headed to Vanderbilt Hospital in Nashville Tennessee and arrived there at 8:30 p.m. In the early hours of August 3rd before I was taken to surgery, my family and I gathered to pray for the donor family. At 4:00 a.m. I was taken for surgery and received a new heart! It was a life-changing moment for me and my family. My road to recovery was a blessed one. I spent three days in ICU and four days in Rest Recovery. In all, I spent seven days in the hospital. The doctor first said that I would have to spend 12 to 15 days in the hospital. Then I was moved in an extended living hotel from August 10th thru 28th, so that I could more easily get to the hospital for my visits and rehabilitation time.

At the beginning of 2012, I decided that it was time to

reach out to the family member of my donor. I hoped and prayed that they would receive it and be willing to answer my letter so that we could get a chance to meet each other. I didn't know their name, or where they lived; I knew that I was grateful for what my donor had done. I wrote the letter and sent it to the Transplant Center who then sent my letter to the Tennessee Donor Services, who forwarded my letter to the donor family.

In January 2012, I sent my letter. Months went by and I didn't hear anything. Finally the last week in May 2012, I received a return letter from Tennessee Donor Services and in the package was a letter from Mrs. Tiki Finlayson and family. What a joy it was for me to read her letter, my eyes just filled up with tears as I read it. What a joy it was for me to hear back from her! Included with her letter were pictures of my donor, Kevin Sunshine Yates. My eyes just filled up with tears and my heart was full of joy!

Now I was able to put a face with my heart donor and my life saving Hero. From that point on we exchanged numbers and started talking with each other, getting dates together so we could meet. Finally we had a date to meet, Saturday, July 7, 2012, in my hometown at Batesville, Mississippi. We met at 5:30 p.m. at the hotel where they were staying. Afterwards, for our meet and greet of both families, we had dinner.

What a joyous and momentous time--for the first time the family was able to hear Kevin's heartbeat! At that dinner we sat and talked and got to know each other. We shared stories, we laughed and cried with each other, but they were joyful tears. We ended our beautiful and joyful weekend with a church service on Sunday morning at Pilgrim Rest Baptist where I'm the pastor. We had a fun filled day of worship service and dinner and fellowship with each other.

From that first meeting up until now we have become one big family that share nothing but love. We have even came up with a new family name which comes from Finlayson, Yates, Bell, and Ellis. We are the "Finyatellisons." I refer to myself as "2-5" because Kevin was 25 years old when he became my Hero.

I'm so thankful for Kevin Sunshine Yates, because if he hadn't made the decision to become an organ donor, I do not know where I would be right now. The family told me that Kevin always wanted to be superhero. I did not know Kevin, nor did I get the chance to see him face to face or shake his hand, but I can feel his presence as his heart beats within my body! THANK YOU KEVIN AND THANK YOU JESUS!!"

OTHER CARRIERS OF KEVIN

I have written to the other recipients numerous times and have not yet received a reply. I do pray for them to have good health and a wonderful quality of life, and to be able to enjoy their families with the second chance from the gift of life Kevin gave. I hope one day I will get to meet them and enjoy a relationship with them as I do with Melvin.

HONORING KEVIN

I just want to say a BIG thank you to Tennessee Donor Services for all of their help and support through this journey. They are wonderful people who aren't there just because it's their job. They truly care about the families of donors. Their staff has gone above and beyond to honor each donor. Kevin has been honored at several events, but there are three that have been my favorites so far.

THANKS FOR GIVING CEREMONY

OCTOBER 13, 2013. This was a special event. Melvin got to come and we spoke together wearing our t-shirts that his church had made. In the ceremony each donor's name and a tribute about them was read Afterward, the families received a gold medallion with hands holding a heart to represent the Gift of Life.

ROSE PARADE

JANUARY 1, 2016. This event was overwhelming to say the least! Kevin had been chosen to represent the state of Tennessee for Donate Life America on their parade float in the Rose Parade! On December 7, 2015, at the media announcement we had a ceremony to finish the Floragraph of Kevin's photo that would be on the float. We had many of our family to attend and of course, Melvin was there and his brother Ervin.

Derek and I flew to Pasadena, California on December 28th. There were over five hundred people at our hotel who were donor family members, living donors, or transplant

recipients. The atmosphere was so sweet. Strangers shared with each other their donor and recipient stories. We all were there to be a part of this event because a loved one gave of themselves so selflessly and became someone's Super Hero.

Many activities had been planned. We got to participate in decorating the float and my highlight was getting to place Kevin's Floragraph on the float. We participated in a sand ceremony where each donor family got to add a color of sand into a large glass container. It was a beautiful sight to see so many families of Super Heroes in one place, and on the other hand, it was so emotional because a loved one had to make the ultimate sacrifice for us to be there.

Donate Life America put on a New Year's Eve party for everyone. We celebrated on Eastern time since we all had to be up and in our special seating the next morning for the parade that the world would be watching!

That 2016 New Year's Day is one I will never forget as we sat in our special seating and saw that float appear in the distance.

As it got closer the cheers, whistles, and screams got louder and louder. And then there it was right in front of us and we all yelled, "DONATE LIFE", and waved our signs and blue and green pompoms. It was so beautiful and there was my baby's smiling face for the world to see! I smiled through the tears, knowing how excited Kevin would have been if he were there.

DONATE LIFE TRANSPLANT GAMES OF AMERICA

JUNE 10-15, 2016. This six day event also was very overwhelming, but in a different way. We were chosen to be a donor family on the Team Tennessee. We were one of three donor families and the rest of our team was transplant recipients who would compete in the games. This event was similar to the Olympics!

My mom, Rene', and I left for Cleveland, Ohio and joined our team there. We had never been on a trip alone together and we cherished getting to have that special time.

There was an Opening Ceremony, multiple events going on all over the city at one time, and Medaling Ceremonies of Gold, Silver, and Bronze.

They also had a Donor Tribute. Outside the huge auditorium there were large posters on easels, one for each donor represented at the Games. WOW! What a sight to see with all the hundreds of posters. And each one was a Super

Hero! Inside there was a gigantic screen where a tribute slideshow was playing with all the donors pictures.

We also participated in a Quilt Square Pinning Ceremony. Each donor family brought a quilt square in memory of their loved one and they were pinned onto an unfinished quilt. Afterwards all the squares would be sewn into a quilt to display at future Transplant Games.

We got to exchange and collect pins from each Team and my first one was from Team Hawaii! There were so many other activities that week, too many to mention. Then the Closing Ceremonies wrapped everything up.

I look forward to many more Donate Life events.

BECOME A SUPER HERO LIKE KEVIN

If Kevin's story of organ donation has inspired you to also be a Super Hero then take a moment to register to be an organ donor too! If you are in the United States of America go to www.BeTheGiftToday.org click "register now" and choose your state to register.

*If you do not live in the United States, search for organ donation in your are*a.

Chapter 4

ROAD TO RECOVERY

DADDY WOKE UP

AFTER DADDY WOKE UP from the coma on Friday, July 29, 2011, every time we went up to visit him my brother, Ty, and I would try to get him to squeeze our hand and to say something, anything. He finally did squeeze our hand. And he would follow us with his eyes. He began to have more and more movement until the nurses ended up having to tie his hands because he would try to pull out his tubes. But still he hadn't spoken a word until Sunday, July 31, 2011, *(the same day Kevin was admitted into the hospital, and was fighting for his life)*. We had been told that it would be best if we didn't tell Daddy that Kevin had been in an wreck. They didn't want the news to upset him and with his head injury it could have caused a setback. So the family had to put happy faces on as if everything was fine before going in to visit with him. Because I was one of the ones that had been there each visit he would have wondered why I wasn't there so I was going to make a quick visit before going around the hall 8 rooms down to be with my Kevin.

I put on my brave, smiling face, went in and said hi to Daddy. And while I was screaming and frantic on the inside, I made small talk. I was only there a couple of minutes and knew I had to get out of there before he realized something was wrong. So I told Daddy that I had to go check on some things and turned to leave. And of all times for him to decide to start talking he said, "Where are you going?" *Really! Now you're going to talk?* I was so surprised he talked, but glad to know that he could after two days of trying to get him to speak. I turned and said I would be back next visit that I just had some things that I needed to check on. And I hurried out the door before he could say anything else. Thankfully there was other family there to try and distract him for me.

QUARANTINED

After that, the doctors decided they would move Daddy that day to the Stepdown ICU on another floor to try and keep him from catching any conversation about Kevin, with him being just down the hall from him. In his new room they had to tell him that the TV wouldn't work due to the fact that he and Kevin were all over the local news on every channel. Tragedy had hit our family twice in a week and because of the nature of the wrecks, we had been interviewed numerous times. We didn't want Daddy finding out what had happened on the news.

After Kevin had died the doctors put Daddy on quarantine, to make it easier for us to have Kevin's funeral and Daddy not ask questions as to why we weren't there to visit him. Daddy's wife, Bobby, was a trooper. She stayed with him the whole time, not able to leave and attend Kevin's funeral. While they were sleeping the morning Kevin died, Bobby was awakened by a voice, and it was Kevin's. She heard Kevin telling his Pipi goodbye. To this day my Daddy cannot talk about that without crying.

On Sunday, August 7, 2011, the quarantine was lifted. Daddy was getting better each day, but still we could not tell him about Kevin. The doctors wanted us to wait until we took Daddy home. It was so difficult to put on a happy face and see him. I had such mixed emotions and I was in a huge fog of grief. I had just buried my baby. But then I would remind myself that this could be worse. I could have had to plan two funerals. I was grateful that I still had my Daddy here with me. He had a long road of recovery ahead of him. And I could get him to do what he was supposed to do when he wouldn't listen to others. I had to do whatever I could to help with him. I knew when he came home I would need to be around, because Daddy is stubborn and headstrong, and I could talk him into doing what the doctors had instructed him to do. I had to be strong, even though I was dying inside.

WHERE IS KEVIN

The day for Daddy to be released couldn't come fast enough for him. Finally, Tuesday, August 9, 2011, he got to go home. We had already decided that whenever that day was, we would all be there to tell him about Kevin. After getting him in the house and settled, he looked around at everyone and I asked him if someone was missing. He said, "Where is Kevin?" I began to tell him what happened and he was so upset that we didn't tell him sooner. He said if he knew he would have left the hospital to go to the funeral. I told him I knew that and it was exactly the reason we didn't tell him, because he was in no condtion to be able to do that.

I then went on to tell him about Kevin being an organ donor. Because of Daddy's head injury this made him really confused. He looked at me with tears in his eyes and said, "I have Kevin's organ and that is why I'm alive?" Even though we assured him that that was not the case, he really struggled with the fact that Kevin died and he is still alive. He said it should have been him.

GETTING CLOSURE WITH KEVIN DYING

The whole reason we video recorded Kevin's service was for Daddy. We asked him if he wanted to watch it and he did not. He told me he would let me know when he was ready. That day did not come until two months later on October 27, 2011, *(which happened to be the same day the Grand Jury charged the drunk driver who killed Kevin).* He and I sat together in my living room as he watched the service on video. I was glad that he was finally able to watch it, but for me it was like I was there all over again. My wounded heart was still mangled and raw. The pain was so intense. All the emotions came like a tsunami overtaking a city. Then I thought about how my Daddy must be feeling. He hadn't experienced the funeral. I began to focus more on comforting my Daddy while tears streamed down my face. When the video was over I asked if he wanted to go to the grave; he did not. And again, he told me he would let me know when he was ready. That day came two months later in

December 2011. Just the two of us went. We didn't say much while we were there. He just stood and stared and we cried together.

DADDY'S NORMAL SELF

Throughout the months of that first year after Daddy's accident he continued to improve and now is as close to 100% of "his normal" as he can be. The only thing that lingers is he can't remember names of some people he has known for years. And yes, he is back on his motorcycle riding again. I am grateful for every day I get to spend with my Daddy.

(Before July 25, 2011 and after August 24, 2011)

Chapter 5

JUSTICE AND MERCY

JUSTICE FOR KEVIN

How can there ever really be justice when someone has been riped from your life due to a 100% preventable crime? Latisha Stephen is responsible for Kevin not been here. What amount of time could she ever serve to justify her actions? Nothing she could do would bring Kevin back, or heal the hurt and grief our family was going through. By the end of this book you will discover there is more than one kind of justice.

LEGAL PROCESS

While we had an amazing district attorney assigned to our case, and in several meetings she explained as much as she could, this was a very frustrating process. If someone who had been through this process before would have explained it to me, I think it might not have caused me so much stress. The first part that was hard for me, due to not knowing, was WHY. Why were we waiting so long for Latisha to be charged, arrested, booked-- just something? I quickly found out that I would definitely have to get used to waiting.

CHOICES

In Tennessee where Kevin was killed, all blood testing goes to one laboratory in Nashville. That alone held up the process for three months. When the toxicology report finally came back the results showed that Latisha's BAC was 0.20 two hours after the time of the wreck, which meant that at the time of the wreck she had a BAC of 0.235! Three times the legal limit of 0.08. With this report, we could finally move forward.

Latisha was booked and had a Grand Jury trial on October 27, 2011. The arraignment was November 11, 2011. We were not permitted to attend either the trail or the arraignment. I did not understand this at all. Should I not be able to be there to be a voice for Kevin? Shouldn't she have to face Kevin's family? However, that time would come later, but not soon enough for our family. We had wanted to be able to have Christmas without the unknown of what sentencing would be.

In between the Grand Jury trail and arraignment, I was interviewed by a local news station during the first public event that our organization 1N3 was participating in on October 29, 2011. (You will hear more about how 1N3 started in a later chapter.) The reporter asked several questions about our mission and what we wanted to accomplish with our message to the community. I was not ready for the last question from the interviewer. He asked, "If you could say anything to the woman who killed your son, what would it be?"

For a moment I was blank. I wasn't expecting THAT question at all. However, I heard God say inside of me, "Now is the time to tell her you forgive her." I thought maybe someone would see the News and tell Latisha, or maybe she would see the News interview herself. So, I looked straight into the camera and said, "Latisha, if you are watching, I want you to know I forgive you." It happened so quickly that there was no time to try and have an angle or think about how it might affect the outcome of the court case. I just knew I needed to say the words publicly for all to hear and see, even though I still didn't feel different about it. I still did not feel forgiveness in my heart.

FIRST COURT DATE

Thursday, January 12, 2012, what a way to start the year! We had been waiting for this day. All the family was going to finally get to see this woman face to face, EXCEPT ME! My husband and I were still in a contract job in Houston as Chaplains at the Harris County Jail. I was not permitted to leave that week. That was one of the most stressful and frustrating days for me, as well as my family.

The defense attorney asked for an extension. When I got the call with the news I was FURIOUS to say the least. They asked for an extension! Kevin didn't get an extension! Where was the fairness in that? We should have gotten a guilty plea. Why would we be put through this horrible nightmare any longer? The inevitable was being delayed.

SECOND COURT DATE

Thursday, March 1, 2012, couldn't come soon enough. We arrived early to get a front row seat, all wearing our 1N3 t-shirts with Kevin's face on them. I was going to see this woman for the first time. I sat and stared at her hoping to lock eyes. I wanted her to see me. I wanted her to see that I wanted justice, but also see forgiveness. But that never happened. She had been instructed early on before the first court date not to look in our direction and to keep her head down.

We were expecting a plea that day, but instead there was new evidence in our favor that our District Attorney needed time to investigate. So again we were delayed in receiving justice for Kevin, and some closure for our family.

THIRD COURT DATE -RESTORATIVE JUSTICE

Thursday, March 29, 2012, changed my life forever. We all gathered outside the courtroom to wait for our docket to be called. I just knew today was the day. We were going to receive justice for Kevin.

While we were waiting, our District Attorney approached us and offered us the opportunity to have a Restorative Justice meeting. I had never heard of it, let alone knew what it was. She explained that we would have the opportunity to sit in a room with Latisha and tell her how her actions impacted our family. And she would be able to respond.

I immediately said, "YES, when can we schedule it?" She said, "TODAY." Today? I was not prepared for today. What would I say? I'm a planner, I needed to write things down. If I was going to get to talk to Latisha, I wanted to make sure I said everything I wanted to say with no "I wish I would have said" moments afterwards. However, if we were going to have the meeting, today was the day. Latisha had to agree to the meeting and she did.

We had less than two hours to prepare. I was sitting outside the courtroom on a bench with my family preparing what we wanted to say. Latisha and her family were only 25 feet away sitting in chair. I had my iPad with me, which was full of pictures of Kevin, and there were audio recordings of his voicemails I had saved. I decided I wanted to make Kevin real to her, because she didn't remember anything about her last two hours before the wreck.

Finally, it was time. Of the family members at court that day, only six of our family chose to go in. There were a couple of family members that didn't trust themselves to be there for fear they would do something they shouldn't. And because of the Restorative Justice meeting being offered in a two-hour time frame, there were others who would have been there that could not make it in time. Following our District Attorney, we all went into the bright, empty room. There was a long bench similar to a church pew up against the wall and we all sat there together. From that bench where we sat to our right there was a table with a few chairs around it, further away across the room looked to be a small court setting, and right in front of us was a line of several chairs about seven feet away. There were no barriers, dividers, or separation of any kind.

Our District Attorney began to give us instructions. To me it sounded like Charlie Brown's parents, (whomp whomp whomp whomp whomp). To this day, I do not remember anything she said. And then in walks a court officer with Latisha, her Dad, and attorney. She and her Dad sat in the chairs in front of us! She sat with her head down, then briefly looked up at each of us and began to cry.

Only three of our family spoke. Kevin's Aunt Crystal, (who you will hear from in the Ripple Effect chapter), went first. It was brutal. Then, Kevin's Mimi, (Rene') spoke next. (You will also hear from her in the Ripple Effect). She didn't say much and did show mercy. Now, it was my turn to speak to this woman who killed my baby boy. Again, I watched this moment from a bird's eye view just like I did when we were in that room in the hospital praying and I said out loud that I forgave her.

I knew that I had to do it here and now. So, I started with, "I'm Kevin's Mom and I want to tell you face to face that I forgive you." I began to show Latisha pictures of Kevin smiling, laughing, and of him in the hospital broken, bloody, and bruised. I told her that she was responsible for taking all of those good times away. Then I played the audio recording of his voice. You could hear the sweetness in his voice. Then I told her that I forgave her again.

I thought I was done. Latisha responded extremely remorseful and cried the whole time. Then I heard God say inside of me. *"You're not done."* I asked God what else He wanted me to do. He said, *"I want you to offer your help to her."* I said, "God, I said I forgave her. Isn't that enough?" He said, *"Do you trust Me?"* I said, "Yes, I do." So, I offered my help to Latisha. I said, "I want to offer my help to you if you will allow me to help you become the woman of God He made you to be. But it's up to you." She was crying and shook her head yes. I knew the prison where she would be incarcerated; I had been a volunteer in the chapel. I told her that I would call the Chaplain and ask for her to connect Latisha with some good people there. I sat back and thought to myself, "You did it! You were obedient." Then again God said, *"You're not done."* I asked Him what else there was to do. And then I heard it......... *"I want you to hug her."* WHAT!?!? HUG HER!! I said, "God I might squeeze too tight and pinch her head off and besides that, they are NOT going to let me do that!" He said, *"You said you trusted Me."* I said, "Okay." Then I asked Latisha if I could hug her and before I got all the words out of my mouth we both stood up and stepped toward each other and were hugging before anyone could try and stop us. We stood there hugging and crying for the longest time. She kept saying, "I'm so sorry! I'm so sorry!" The first thing that comes to most people's mind when someone says I'm sorry is, "It's okay." BUT it was not okay and would never be okay. So, all I could think to say is, "We will go forward from here."

When we finally stopped hugging, I looked around the room and most everyone was teary eyed as we were leaving. It was a very emotional moment that I will never forget. It left me feeling drained and empowered all at the same time. There was something that broke off of me and healing began for both Latisha and me that day as well as the others that were there.

SENTENCING DAY

Tuesday, April 3, 2012, was the day I insisted that we have our last court date, because the court wanted to have it on April 2, 2012. We already had a full day of plans that had been prepared for weeks. On April 2nd we released a song and video tribute to Kevin, and had a birthday party and balloon release at the cemetery for what would have been his 26th birthday. We had breakfast at IHOP where Kevin had many friends. And dinner at Buffalo Wild Wings where he worked and had left that fateful night. Again, it was an extremely emotional and draining day. And now, on this day, we will finally get justice for Kevin.

We arrived at the courthouse and gathered out in the foyer area. Then I saw Latisha in the distance. She walked toward the courtroom with her family. I walked up to her and asked how she was doing. And immediately we had officers and attorneys gathered around as if to try and break up a fight. She looked at them and said, "We're okay." As they all walked away one by one we began to talk. And for two hours while we waited for our docket to be called out in the foyer, our family and Latisha's family talked together.

Latisha and I had our picture made together, and she made a video for us to use with 1N3 at our presentations. She expressed wanting to be part of the solution to the crime of drinking and driving.

She was sentenced that day. Eight years for vehicular homicide and six years supervised probation after the eight years for reckless endangerment with a deadly weapon (the Jeep). The judge allowed us to show mercy in a small way by negotiating that Latisha would serve at least 20% instead of the state requirement of 30% of her time before she would be eligible for parole. She turned and spoke to our family after the judge sentenced her. She took full responsibility for her actions, and then was taken into custody to serve her time.

As our family and Latisha's family left that day, there really were no winners, only losers. Everyone felt loss and separation from a loved one that we all were going to have to learn to live with. Worst of all, Latisha would have to live with the reality of knowing she killed Kevin and it could have been prevented. I would not wish that on anyone.

I do understand that some of you may be thinking eight months from start to finish for this case seems like a long time when the evidence was plain to see, but for others of you who may be going through or have been through this same process, you may be asking how it happened this quickly. Our case was not the "norm" in this situation. I don't really know why our process was only eight months, other than prayer.

We had a lot of people praying "JUSTICE FOR KEVIN" around the world. Yes, there were days I was extremely frustrated, and wanted to "nail her to the wall." But what good would that really do in the end? There are no winners in this process. I prayed that God would bring good out of this tragedy and told God I trusted Him over and over. All I know is prayer changes things. And God works behind the scenes when you put the situation in His hands and let Him.

IS THIS ALL KEVIN'S LIFE IS WORTH

It had been nine months since our last court date and Latisha had been sentenced and incarcerated. She and I had written letters back and forth. I had seen her a few times while at the prison volunteering at the chapel. And she was in an intense group called Therapeutic Community and was doing well. We were trying to find our way with each other. She had expressed wanting to be part of the solution, and I believed her.

On Friday, January 11, 2013, I was sitting in my office at 1N3 and volunteers were busy working and my phone rang. I answered and the lady on the other end of the line stated her name. She began to tell me that Latisha would be coming up for parole in March and that I needed to write an Impact Statement for her file. She asked if I would be attending the parole hearing. I just sat there stunned and speechless. I told her I had not been informed that she was even eligible for parole yet.

While I knew about "good time" from volunteering in correctional facilities for many years, I had not really thought about the sentence reduction credits for good behavior where Latisha's time was concerned. She only had to serve 20% of her time before she was eligible for parole. And with getting up to sixteen days a month off her sentence for every month that she had good behavior, it meant eleven months after she was incarcerated, she was eligible.

Well, after the lady explained this to me she asked again if I would be attending the parole hearing. I told her I would. And she said, "Okay so you will be coming in opposition." I said, "No". She said, "Let me explain this to you. There are only two options; in support or opposition. So you are coming in opposition." I said, "No, I'm coming in support." She said, "Honey, I don't think you understand." I said, "I understand what this means. I am coming in support for Latisha to get out of prison." Then she was quiet on the other end for a few seconds. Finally she said, "Alright, I put you down in support."

When I hung up the phone I just sat there quietly with all kind of thoughts running through my head. I looked up and said, "God, REALLY? Is Kevin's life not worth more than eleven months?" He said, "You said you trusted Me." I said, "I do trust You, but eleven months?" He said, "*You said when I knew she was ready to get out you would be fine with it. You said you trust Me*?" I said, "Yes, I trust You. If You know she is ready to get out, then I'll be fine with it. But I have no idea what to say to the Parole Board." He said, "Sit down and write what you hear." So I did. And there were a lot of emotions and tears as I wrote.

During next two months all I could think about was Latisha getting out of prison. What would that look like? Part of her sentencing was that she had to volunteer ninety days with 1N3 after she was released. How would we make this work? I just couldn't stop thinking about it.

ASKING FOR RELEASE

MARCH 13, 2013. Early that Wednesday morning we left Chattanooga headed for Nashville to the Tennessee Prison for Women's maximum security facility. There was only four of our family who chose to attend the Parole Hearing. We arrived and waited in line to be searched and patted down at the security check point. After completing that process we were taken to the visitor's gallery, which was full of people who were also waiting for their turn before the Parole Board.

We saw Latisha's family and went over to greet them. In total there were twenty-one of us there for her hearing. All in support! We were instructed to sit in a certain area to wait for our turn. I happened to be sitting directly in front of Latisha's youngest son, now twelve years old. I turned around and asked how he was doing and made small talk. Then I asked him if he was praying for his mom to get to come home. Very confidently he said, "Yes, and I know my momma is coming home." I told him I was praying for that too. I turned back around in my seat and prayed, "God, You have to get her out of here now! This baby is believing You will do this. You can't let him down."

CHOICES

It was almost time for our appointment for the hearing and Latisha was brought in. Everyone greeted her and visited for a few minutes until we were called for her hearing. All twenty-one of us filed in with Latisha. She had three of her family speaking on her behalf and ME. The four of us sat on the front row right behind Latisha. She sat at a table in front of a huge screen. The Parole Board was in another room being video conferenced into our room. (I'm guessing for security reasons.) They came on the screen and spoke to Latisha and asked her questions. It was time for her character witnesses to speak. Her three family members spoke on her behalf, telling why she should be released to come home. Then it was my turn. I was so nervous. All eyes were on me, the mother of the man she had killed. I'm sure they were all preparing themselves for what they would hear from me, but not even I was prepared for how my words would sound in that moment. As I read my statement to the Parole Board I watched as they lowered their heads down, putting their hand up on their forehead, with a pen in the other hand as if to write on a legal pad. I could tell they did not want anyone to see their tears.

MY VICTIM IMPACT STATEMENT

"I too am guilty of killing someone. It was a very brutal death of an innocent person who asked His Father before He died to forgive me for my crime. And His Father granted the request and today we have a personal relationship, He loves me as His own, and doesn't hold what I did over my head. Who am I to not extend that same forgiveness? The person I killed was Jesus. He died because of my sin and God forgave me. I am so thankful for that forgiveness. To show my

gratitude, I tell the story with the hope of showing people that forgiveness is possible and that it truly brings freedom.

So when I was faced with Latisha killing my son, Kevin, I knew I had to make the choice to extend that same forgiveness that was given to me. As a result of my choice to forgive Latisha, we have started to form a relationship that I believe will change many lives through spreading awareness of the dangers and consequences of drunk driving with the organization, 1N3, which we started after Kevin's death.

Latisha was kind enough to record a video for us on her sentencing day that we have used at our presentations and events and has been seen by hundreds of thousands of people and she has already made an impact along with us. And her family has been involved while she has been here at TPW.

I am certainly not excusing Latisha's choice to drink and drive. It was wrong. She knew the consequences before she took the first drink on the night of July 30, 2011. This was 100% preventable not only by Latisha, but by those who were with her that night. The homeowner of the party she attended who supplied alcoholic punch; the bar she went to after the party and left from; the friend who made her pull over because Latisha was driving so badly and was scaring her and someone else drove the rest of the way to the friend's house; the person who drove the rest of the way to the friend's house who got out of the jeep left the keys in the ignition and left it running, then let her drive away knowing she was not in any condition to be driving. They got home safe, but weren't concerned about anyone else. In my eyes they are just as responsible for Kevin's death. If just one of them had taken the key, called a cab, or even driven Latisha where she needed to go, Kevin would be here today.

Kevin's family and Latisha's family became one in three who are impacted by drunk driving on July 31, 2011, when Kevin met Latisha on Hwy 153 at 1:48 a.m. On August 1, 2011, at 8:57a.m., Kevin's family and friends were given a "life sentence" without Kevin here on earth. We are forever on an up and down rollercoaster of feeling; however, we have chosen to take a horrible tragedy and use it to bring a change and hopefully save other families from being forced to become 1N3. Together we can make a difference.

It has come to my attention that Latisha will not be able to travel outside Hamilton County while on parole once she is released. I am requesting that she be granted permission to travel under my supervision to 1N3's presentation and events. I feel that with Latisha by my side helping to share our story, we can make a bigger impact on our neighborhood, community, state and nationwide.

Thank you,

Tiki Finlayson, Kevin 'Sunshine" Yates' Mother"

When I finished there was a long pause of silence in the room. Then one of the Board members spoke up and said Latisha's file would be reviewed and that all they heard would be taken into consideration. And the hearing was over. We were instructed to leave the room, and we had a few more minutes to visit with Latisha before we were escorted out to the check point area to leave.

On the ride home we felt positive that parole would be granted. We understood that there were a lot of restrictions to be on parole and many hoops to jump through. And if she missed just once she would be sent right back to prison to complete her time as if she had never been out on parole. I had all kind of scenarios running through my head of what we could do together, standing side by side.

Two weeks later we got the news. Latisha was granted parole! She was the first inmate in the state of Tennessee to have ever made parole on the first time before the Board with the charge of Vehicular Manslaughter by Intoxication. However, there were some requirements that had to be met before her release. She had a couple of classes to finish at the prison, and then she would be moved to The Next Door transition center in Chattanooga for four months.

ONLY "HALF WAY" HOME

JULY 11, 2013, Latisha had met her requirements at the Tennessee Prison for Women and was moved to The Next Door in Chattanooga, Tennessee, which is a transition center (halfway house). I knew there would be an adjustment time and a waiting period before she could have visitors. I had toured the facility with a few other family members prior to Latisha being moved there. I had asked them about volunteering there, and about visiting Latisha when she was there. They told me that would be a possibility. I would find out later that was not the case. I had hoped to be able to visit a few times for us to start finding our way for the two of us to working together. But it would be delayed. However, I trusted God's timing with it all.

590 DAYS

NOVEMBER 13, 2013. Finally the day came when Latisha would be released. I did have mixed emotions, but was more nervously excited than anything. She would be released later in the day. I had been communicating with her family who was picking her up. It was important for me to get the opportunity to see her. We had a picture on sentencing day and I wanted a picture on release day.

She called me on her way home and we talked for several minutes and set up a time to meet. For me, the next couple of hours felt as if they were crawling. I desperately wanted to see her and hug her again. It was the oddest feeling. I kept thinking to myself, this is NOT normal. But then again nothing about my life had been normal since July 31, 2011, and would never be normal again. Why was I feeling this way? I was nervous that Latisha would think I was crazy. I later found out that she did, but glad I was crazy enough to want to have a relationship with her after what she had done. My mind was bombarded with all kinds of scenarios. We were only meeting for a few minutes, but that was a good start.

On that cold evening, I sat alone in my truck waiting for Latisha and her family to arrive in the empty parking lot. I was daydreaming of all we could do together to make an impact for the good in this world. As all the scenes rolled through my mind their vehicle pulled into the parking lot, drove up and parked beside me. With a big smile on her face she got out and we hugged. We  did get our picture and talked for a little while. We planned to talk over the phone and meet to spend some time together at her home the following Monday.

After nineteen months of incarceration, finally we could go forward and make plans to work together for the good. Together we could make a difference and impact the world. This chapter was closed and we would write a new one together.

CHOICES

Chapter 6

CHOICES MATTER

DID YOU EVER IMAGINE making that decision would become as powerful, life changing and freeing for so many people as it has? I get asked this question a lot! And my answer is "No." Little did I know in the beginning of this journey that "Choices Matter" would become our coin phrase.

Before this horrible, life-altering event I knew the importance of my choices and the impact that they have on me and others around me. BUT I never really thought about it the way I do now. Most children are raised to know right from wrong and the consequences of our choices according to our parents or care-givers definition. Children are born without that filter. You don't have to teach a child to act bad, lie, be selfish, etc. They must be taught to act good, tell the truth, be kind, and share with others. If not, they will be wild and unruly. Sometimes there are those children that are raised so strict that when they do get out on their own, they throw all caution to the wind. They don't care about the consequences of the choices they make.

We are the captain of our ship. We are the only one who can determine our choices; until someone makes such a severe choice that their right to make their own choices is taken away. As children we get toys taken away, as teenagers we are grounded, as adults we face probation, jail or prison.

LIFE SENTENCE

The choices we make every day are important. They impact people around us, our family, friends, school mates, co-workers, and complete strangers. Before July 31, 2011, Latisha and I had no idea that each other even existed. But today we live a life-sentence together.

My life-sentence, because of Latisha's choice to drink and drive, is never having another day with Kevin. Never another birthday, he is forever 25. We celebrate his birthday at the cemetery by his little piece of land (his grave) and release balloons. We do something fun that he liked to do, and we go have a cupcake for Kevin.

We will never celebrate another holiday with Kevin. Christmas is the hardest because it was Kevin's favorite. We had a tradition of all the kids coming home to my house and we decorated the tree together, spent the day just being with each other and having fun. Kevin loved to help Tom put the lights on the tree. Because he was so tall (6 feet 5 inches), he could reach all the way around the tree! Our first Christmas without Kevin, we tried to continue our tradition, but it ended up being a heart-wrenching day for me, not to mention not very fun for anyone else. I just couldn't handle it. So for the first three years we didn't have a Christmas tree at my house. On the fourth year I wanted to try again because I had my first grandbaby. I wanted her to have a tree at Gigi and Pappy's house. I decided to buy a pre-lit tree and new decorations. As I was deciding the theme of our new tree, unknowingly, several people randomly would post Batman Christmas trees on my social media! I thought to myself, "Kevin would have loved to have a Batman Christmas tree!" That was a way to bring a little of Kevin into our Christmas. We have had a Batman tree ever since.

I'll never get to sit and see Kevin stand and watch the love of his life walk down the aisle to be married. I'll never get to see him be a Daddy. I'll never get to be a Gigi and hold his babies. I'll never get to see him accomplish his life's goals and dreams. I'll never get to see him grow old. I could fill up numerous books with the "I'll never . . ."

Latisha's life-sentence for her choice to drink and drive is knowing that she killed Kevin and took all of that away from me and his family and friends. I can't imagine waking up every day knowing that I was responsible for taking someone's life away because of my very irresponsible choice--that was 100% preventable! Her choice not only impacted our lives, it also impacted her and her children, family and friends. Countless people on both sides were effected. Even the First Responders who worked the wreck were impacted. Station 19 (green team) knew Kevin from when he worked at Buffalo Wild Wings. They had been there several times in the past when Kevin waited on them. The night of the wreck was no different. Kevin had waited on them just hours earlier and now they were cutting his van away to extract him and trying to save his life. The Emergency Room workers were impacted. They knew Latisha because she worked at the hospital. The list just kept growing of the people who were impacted all because of one choice to drink and drive.

CHOICES WE WERE FORCE TO MAKE

Latisha's one choice forced our family to have to make choices we should have not had to make. We had to walk through a funeral home full of empty caskets and choose the best one for Kevin. We had to walk through the cemetery full of graves looking at all the empty spaces and choose the perfect place to bury my baby. (By the way, there is no perfect place.) I had to go through Kevin's clothes and choose his last outfit. He wore something Batman a lot, so Batman it was. We had to choose songs for his service. The list of choices and tasks that I was forced to make just kept growing.

THE CHOICE I WAS NOT FORCED TO MAKE

The one choice I made on my own that I was not forced to make has changed my whole life. As a matter of fact, it saved my life! I know I would not be here today. I would have grieved myself to death. That choice was FORGIVENESS!

Now I promise I am as human as you are. Forgiving the person that just killed my youngest son was NOT what I felt like doing. I wanted to do something completely opposite that would have put me behind bars, and caused my family even more heartache and grief. But forgiveness is not a feeling. It is a choice. I knew in order for me to be able to use this horrible tragedy for good I had to forgive. I wanted to go and tell everyone who would listen about how "Choices Matter" and the consequences of the actions that follow those choices. I wanted it to be educational and informative, and not come across angry or finger pointing at anyone. And forgiveness was what would get me there.

CHOICES MATTER

I made my choice while we were still at the hospital with Kevin, but it was several months before I felt any different inside. I would tell people all the time about Kevin's story and still feel horrible. And finally one day I was sharing with someone and noticed something was different. I knew I had unlocked the prison cell that Latisha's actions had thrown me in. I knew every time I shared with people I was a step closer to being completely free of the bitterness and ugliness inside. I was determined to not let Latisha's choice control my life and kill me. It killed Kevin and I knew he wouldn't want me to crawl in a corner and die. He would want me to change the world. Because of my choice to forgive, so many doors of opportunity have opened to make an impact with Kevin's story.

As I said earlier the choices we make are impacting people all around us. And the choice Latisha made impacted so many of Kevin's family, friends, and even someone he had only met once. I could fill up countless books from people who were impacted by Kevin's death. However, I have only chosen a few, and in chapter 9 you will read a few of them. Their stories are the ripple effects of one choice to drink and drive.

In this next chapter I will share more about grief and forgiveness.

CHOICES

Chapter 7

GRIEF AND FORGIVENESS

YOU MAY BE ASKING YOURSELF why I would combine grief and forgiveness in the same chapter. Well, it is because I have discovered that where there is grief, there is an opportunity to forgive. In this chapter I will share some of what I have learned about grief and forgiveness, as well as share how forgiveness has played a role in the healing process for me. I realized while writing this book and collecting my notes on both subjects that I had enough for a book on both topics, so I have chosen to share the highlights. I am considering writing a book on both to be able to share more of what I have learned in hopes to help others better understand and work through the process.

GRIEF THROUGH MY EYES

I never really thought much about grief before Kevin died. I did have people close to me that had died and it affected me deeply. I did grieve, but didn't really think about it. It was just part of life. Right? However, when Kevin died, that grief was horrible, and I felt it was unbearable most of the time! There is a saying that I have heard, "There is a label for a spouse who loses their spouse, a widow or widower. There is a label for a child who loses their parents, an orphan. But there is no label for a parent who loses a child, because there are no words to describe the pain." And that is exactly right.

It was like I was in a fog that never lifted. I couldn't see past the moment I was in and I just started each day trying to make it through to the next. While I had already chosen to forgive Latisha, my thoughts, emotions, and feelings did not agree with my choice yet. I missed Kevin terribly to say the least. But I continued to tell God I trusted Him to get me through each day. The pain was so intense that every morning I would wake up and say, "God, can it be today? Can I leave here?" I hardly had any will to live. On the other hand, knowing the pain I was going through, I didn't want my family to have to deal with the pain of losing me as well as Kevin.

I want to share a little background of my life before Kevin left. It was very full. My husband, Tom, and I were overseeing our ministry, Pursuing Purpose. We had 120 volunteers and 86 service times in 8 different jail and prison facilities each month. We were also traveling to Texas several times a year to partner with Mike Barber Ministries to do huge prison events. With all of this, we were trying to juggle our home life with our three adult children and one teenager. In 2010 we were offered the opportunity for a one-year contract to be on staff with Mike Barber, a former Houston Oilers football player, (who started prison ministry after he retired from his football career), at the Harris County Jail. It had three buildings housing seven-thousand inmates on any given day. They wanted us to come and train them on the system we had created to minister day to day behind the walls and bars. And we would learn to do the large "Weekend of Excitement" events that they put on each month. It was a great way to expand our reach behind the walls of jails and prisons. In February of 2011, we packed what we needed for an apartment and headed to Houston, Texas, leaving our two adult sons to live in our home in Chattanooga, Tennessee. Each month we would drive back and forth, three weeks in Houston and one week in Chattanooga to monitor the activity of Pursuing Purpose. This was a big change and adjustment for us, but we were managing it well and having fun doing it. However, we had no idea of the adjustment our whole family would have to make just a few months later. I would never have thought in a million years how upside down our lives were getting ready to be. On July 26, 2011, when my Daddy's wreck happened; then five days later on July 31st Kevin's wreck occurred, and thirty-one hours and nine minutes later on August 1, 2011, Kevin was gone.

Five weeks after Kevin died, still in a huge fog; I flew out of Chattanooga, and was back in Houston working my Chaplain's position at the Harris County Jail. It was my first day back and I had gone through the security check point, and gotten on the elevator going to our office on the sixth floor. The substance abuse counselor was already on the elevator with her cart. She was going to lead a class with the inmates. I noticed on her cart a book called "The Grief Recovery Handbook". I asked her where she got the book and she began to tell me that she used it in her substance abuse classes because when addicts are trying to start a new life without drugs or alcohol there is grief due to the separation from something that has been a part of their life for so long. I was amazed. I had never thought of grief being attached to anything other than death.

I told her I would like to buy one and ask where I could get the book. I then shared with her why I wanted it. She gave me her condolences and then said she would bring me one before the end of the day. And she did. I was excited to get home and start reading it. I wanted and needed some relief. After getting home I realized it was not a faith-based book, so I laid it on the end table in the living room and there it sat while I struggled to get through each day. I thought that no secular book would do me any good. I was hanging onto God and His Word that I had learned before this tragedy. I didn't want to waste my time with something that I thought would not help. I continued to plug my earbuds in almost 24/7 and listened to worship music. I was in such a fog that I could not even read my Bible. The only words I could find to pray in English were, "God, I don't understand but I trust You to bring good out of this." And the music kept me going.

A LITTLE SIDE NOTE

I was taught to live by faith and trust God, and that if anything was not faith-based or visibly God-centered to stay away from it. Well, since then I have discovered that God can use whatever avenue He chooses in order to do whatever He needs to bring healing in your life as well as open your eyes to the purpose He has for you. I learned to not try and put God in a box. He can do so much more in your life if you open your mind and heart to the unlimited possibilities of what He can do. Take it from me; don't waste time by ignoring the very thing God wants to use to help you.

I would pull myself out of the bed each morning knowing that if I continued to lay there I would give up completely. I would take my cup of coffee, and my Bible, and find a spot for some alone time with God. My favorite place was outside. It was like I felt closer to Him there. The warm days were ideal. On chilly days I would wrap up in a blanket. And on cold days I would sit inside by a window, so I could look out. I would open my Bible and start to read, but day after day was the same. I would stare at the page and my brain couldn't comprehend anything. So, I would sit and listen for a while. Some days I would hear God speak to me on the inside about whatever I was seeing that day as I looked at my surroundings. I would write down what I heard in a journal. The words would always bring comfort to my shattered, raw, and weary soul. On the days that I didn't hear His voice I would put my earbuds in, play my worship music, and sing through the tears.

Each morning when I headed out to have my alone time I would pass by the book still sitting on the end table in my living room where I left it. I would hear the words, "Pick it up and read it". I would think to myself, "There is no use in reading it. It can't help me". This went on every day for two months. Finally, one day I heard, "Just read the first few pages". I was desperate! I thought I was literally going crazy. I had so many feelings all at the same time. I cried all the time. Tears would just stream down my face and I couldn't stop them. Sometimes when Tom wasn't home (which was rare because we worked together and lived together 24/7) I would put my face in my pillow and scream to the top of my voice just to try and relieve the pain. Even though I had chosen to forgive, my thoughts, feelings and emotions were not on board yet. Kevin had been ripped out of mine and my family's lives. He was my baby boy. I wanted to die, and I didn't want to die all at the same time.

Finally, one evening after a long day at the jail, I walked by the end table in the living-room headed to the bedroom and I heard, "PICK IT UP AND READ THE FIRST FEW PAGES!" It was so loud in my head. So, I carried it to the bedroom, laid across the bed, and opened the book. I read two pages, and realized I WAS NOT CRAZY! What I was feeling was normal! And I was so upset with myself for not reading it when I brought it home. I felt like I had just lost two months of progress I could have made. From that time on I read the book every available minute I could. I knew if I continued to do the exercises that it suggested that eventually I just might find my way out of this dark hole I had been thrown into. While doing this, I continued to have my alone time with God and my Bible and eventually was able to read it again. My worship music, my alone time with God, and The Grief Recovery Handbook saved my life!

FORGIVENESS PLAYS A ROLE IN HEALING GRIEF

For me, I worked through the grief and forgiveness process together. Both emotions, the grief and unforgiveness, would come in waves. The best way I can think to explain it is like walking on the sandy beach heading for the ocean. You walk out into the water and the further you go, the bigger the waves are. You stand and watch for the waves to come. Some you can float over, others you must jump to get some height to go over them. But then there are the ones that crash on top of you and roll you on the bottom of the ocean floor, and you must figure out which way is up. You fight to get your feet on the ocean floor and push your way to the surface for air. The waves are unpredictable! There may even be one crashing on you again as you reach the surface and you fill your lungs with air again just before being slammed to the bottom again.

Grief and unforgiveness are just like the waves. You can be doing okay one minute and a word someone says, a clip in a television show or movie, a memory, (and the list keeps going), can send you into a tailspin of emotions that you have to figure out what to do with. For myself, I decided to hit them head on. I worked through the feelings when they came no matter where I was or who might be around. I allowed myself to feel what I was feeling. I didn't try to ignore or push them down. (That is like trying to hold a beach ball under water. It will keep surfacing every time.) I didn't allow the grief to keep me isolated. I would go to work, to the store, church, or wherever with tears streaming down my face. I didn't care if it made people uncomfortable. This is exactly what it does. I discovered that most people do not know how to handle individuals who are walking through grief. They say stupid things, because they don't know what else to say. (However, that is a whole book of experiences, so we will save that for another book.) I didn't let that keep me from going out of my house and being around people. I refused to imprison myself. Crying was just what was happening most of the time. And I learned from the Grief Recovery Handbook that I didn't ever have to apologize for my feelings or for crying. So, I didn't, and still don't apologize for my tears.

Even though I made a choice to forgive, that didn't stop the unforgiveness from trying to come on me. Those waves that tried to come were fierce. My head would scream at me the reasons why I should not forgive Latisha. I would feel anger and rage start at my feet and try and rise and overtake me. I had to fight with everything in me to not give in to the feelings. I would say out loud to myself, "NO! I chose to forgive!" I had to redirect the feelings of anger and rage toward my choice of forgiveness. Speaking what you want to see in your life until you believe it is the key. When you speak, your mind must shut up. In the beginning it was second by second, then minute by minute, then hour by hour, until it was day by day. IT WAS NOT EASY! It was the hardest fight of my life so far. And I hope I never have to experience anything like that again, but I know that if I do, I have the ability in me to get through it. I just have to choose to.

 I know that if I had not chosen to forgive I would not be here today. I would have grieved myself to death, literally. I would have let bitterness; depression, anger, and rage control me because of the grief and unforgiveness. Instead I chose not to give up on me. It wasn't an overnight thing. It took months before I even felt different when I would tell someone my story and say, "I chose to forgive". Then one day I was sharing with someone and said those four little words and I finally felt something shift. I knew then that it was working. And it gave me the courage to want to continue moving forward.

 The forgiveness was a big part in healing my grief in addition to reading The Grief Recovery Handbook. And to get to the feeling of forgiveness I had to have a lot of talks with God. There were too many days to count that He carried me through my day. It was all I could do to even utter those four little words, but I knew if I didn't it would be the end for me. Forgiveness was a matter of life and death for me. People thought I was crazy, and like I said earlier, I thought I was going crazy. But I knew that Kevin would not want me to stop living. He would want me to live life to the fullest like he did, and to not take a day for granted because we are not promised tomorrow. I know Kevin would have been the first one to forgive had he stayed here on this earth. So, I chose to fight for me and I'm here writing this book today in hopes that what I have been through encourages someone that they can get through whatever it is they are going through with God's help.

Your body was never designed to handle the toll that unforgiveness will have on you. There is scientific evidence that we are wired for love. We were never meant to carry the weight of unforgiveness and the stress it brings. It will bring on chronic illnesses and suck the life out of you if it's left alone. This quote is so true, "Unforgiveness is like drinking poison and expecting the other person to die". It's not possible for that to happen. Unforgiveness brings depression and anxiety while forgiveness will bring peace. Choose to fight for yourself. I did.

Do I still grieve now? Some may think I do when I have what I call "Kevin moments". (They used to be Kevin days.) These are times when out of nowhere something triggers a sweet memory and I smile and then start to cry. I don't know if it's grief because it doesn't stay around long. I've heard it said that the pain from grief is the cost of loving someone so much. And that may be true. Yes, I love Kevin so much and he is still a huge part of my life, just not physically. And that is what I miss so bad it hurts. Those hurts are what lets me know that he is still alive in my heart and that is okay. God holds my hand through those moments and reassures me that Kevin is now in my future.

CHOICES

Do I ever wish I had not forgiven, or want to just stop forgiving Latisha? The answer is no. I'm so thankful I chose to forgive her. Even though I couldn't see it in the beginning, now I can see the good and the positive impact that has come from it. I hear about the countless people who have heard our story and said, "If she can forgive the woman who killed her son, I can certainly forgive the person who hurt me." We have started a Forgiveness Movement! What are you waiting for? I promise you it is so worth it!

Here are some quotes and thoughts on forgiveness and being unforgiving.

QUOTES

Here are some of the quotes I have read that have encouraged me.

"Forgiveness is not something we do, it is who we are." Piero Ferucci

"We all agree that forgiveness is a beautiful idea until we have to practice it." C.S. Lewis

"It may be infinitely less evil to murder a man then to refuse to forgive him. The former may be the act in a moment of passion, the latter is the heart's choice." George McDonald

"To be a Christian means to forgive the inexcusable, because God has forgiven the inexcusable in you." C.S. Lewis

WHAT FORGIVENESS IS NOT

Forgiveness is NOT making light of or excusing the situation.

Forgiveness is NOT pushing down the negative emotions. Confront them and deal with them as they come.

Forgiveness is NOT reconciliation. If a person is dangerous, you do not have to have them in your life.

Forgiveness is NOT saying there are no consequences and no justice.

Forgiveness is NOT trust. Trust must be earned.

WHAT FORGIVENESS IS AND DOES

Forgiveness is canceling the debt. Forgiveness is truly wishing well to the person who hurt you, (and mean it), but it does not require that we like that person or have to ever be around them again.

Forgiveness is refusing to be consumed by the wrong done to you, refusing to allow that person to live rent free in your mind and destroying your peace of mind.

Forgiveness heals painful memories and can restore health.

Forgiveness relieves anxiety and depression.

Forgiveness restores peace with God and man. When you truly forgive, the feelings and emotions you experience are indescribable. You know you are making progress and have truly forgiven when you think differently about the person or situation and you feel peace.

UNFORGIVENESS

Unforgiveness is being stuck in the moment of the hurt or loss. It is on replay and you experience the hurt over and over. It robs you of living your best life.

Unforgiveness is a bomb that continually blows up. There is no countdown clock to warn you when it will blow, but you know it will. If you were to find a bomb, you would yell for everyone to run and get as far away as possible and take cover. You wouldn't want them to be hurt in the blast. When we hold onto unforgiveness there will be loved ones who will be hurt. They are in the blast radius of your unforgiving attitude and behavior. You can stop the bomb. But will you use that ability? It starts with saying, "I forgive...."

The painful thoughts, feelings, and emotions that are caused by hurt and trauma will not heal if you avoid forgiving and dealing with the situation. It will be on replay in your mind until you do. Many people who choose not to forgive turn to drugs and alcohol to numb the pain. One problem with that is whatever you were trying to escape is there waiting on you when you come down off your high or sober up. We must deal with the hurts to live our best life.

When you carry unforgiveness from the past into the present it will affect your future. Unforgiveness will bring toxic thoughts, feelings, emotions, and behaviors into your life. It is like a cancer just eating away at your life and left to itself, it will kill you. Choose to live!

FORGIVENESS IS FREEDOM!
THE CHOICE IS YOURS

Chapter 8

1N3

A MISSION IS BORN

ONE IN THREE OF US are impacted by drunk driving was the statistic in 2011 that we now use as the name of our organization. During our time in the hospital, while Kevin was fighting for his life, Derek said, "We need to do something to bring more awareness and change this statistic." We talked about it and threw around a few ideas thinking Kevin would be a part of it. We didn't know how big of a part he would play in our idea. But right then, our focus was getting Kevin better, home, and recovered. It was only a few hours later that we would find out Kevin wouldn't physically be a part of our plan for 1N3. Our mission is to bring drunk driving awareness to the world and save other families from starting this new journey in a club we were forced to be in.

While we were in our aftermath phase planning for a funeral, we had 1N3 on our minds and in our conversations. Even Kevin's remembrance cards that Derek designed and made were bringing awareness. Although we were grieving and trying to make sense of what had just happened we knew that we wouldn't wish what we were going through on anyone, and we wanted to make a difference.

After Kevin's funeral we were consumed with getting our new mission going. The sooner we could get out there with our story, the sooner we could save other families from this pain. We were researching, talking about what we wanted to do, and how we wanted to do it. We were talking about what our name for the non-profit would be. To this day I really cannot tell you what some of the names were that were flying around among all of us. But I can tell you that none of them really worked for us except 1N3, which was my brother Ty's idea. Derek liked it too. My brother said, "Well that is who we are now, we are a part of that statistic. We are one in three, we have been impacted." I wasn't sure about the name in the beginning, but the more we talked about it and comments were made stating, "We are one in three" or "I am one in three", it just kind of stuck. And just like that we had our name, 1N3. The website is www.iam1N3.org because I AM 1N3. I've been impacted. *(Ironically we found out later that one in three people are also waiting for a life saving organ.)*

My first public opportunity to speak was August 19, 2011, and I took it. It was less than three weeks after putting my son in the ground, it was still very fresh, raw, and my heart was ripped open and bleeding, BUT I wanted to save someone else from this pain that I thought would eventually kill me. I took every opportunity to share my 1N3 story on a large or small scale, even with store clerks in the checkout lines. I didn't care, I was on a mission.

Our planning made progress daily. Family and friends were

joining our efforts and helping any way they could. Then finally we had t-shirts, signs, banners, and a borrowed tent to do our first event at a Fall Festival on October 29, 2011. It was less than three months after we were all forced to start this horrible journey in this "club" none of us ever thought in a million years we would be in. One of the local TV stations heard about what we were doing and came out just to interview us and cover the story. The reporter asked a lot of questions about Kevin, the wreck, what I knew about the case, and then he asked, "If you could say anything to the drunk driver what would you want to say?" I was not prepared for that question. I knew I had made a choice to forgive her on July 31st and had been telling everyone that I forgave her, so I thought now was as good a time as any to tell her publicly. Maybe someone she knew would see it and tell her, or maybe she would see it herself. So this is what I said.

"Latisha, I want you to know that I forgive you. And that I just want you to be able to change your life through all of this and to realize that it was a bad choice. And hopefully you'll never make a choice like that again. And that you'll tell others that it's not worth it to drink and drive."

I had no idea if Latisha saw it or not. Either way it was my choice and no matter what, I was determined to not let what she did control me. It was my responsibility to work through the process and saying it on TV for the world to see through a social media post was one way to push the process for me.

That first event was a great start. And with that we started promoting 1N3 on social media and telling anyone who would listen. We continued to research and make plans. One of those plans was to have Kevin's van on a trailer and haul it to our events and presentations.

CHOICES

KEEPING MANGLED METAL

It seemed as though it would take an act of congress to get possession of the van. It was evidence in the case, and after that it would be released to the insurance company to pay off the loan Kevin had. Most everyone I talked to thought I was crazy for wanting to have his van. But I had been on the evidence lot and seen it up close and it screamed very loudly and made a statement without a single word. I wanted people to see his right shoe stuck under the gas pedal (it is still there to this day, we cannot get it loose), the crushed soda can, his keys still hanging in the ignition, and the list goes on and on.

We were finally approved to have the van released to us when it was no longer needed for evidence. Now all we needed was a trailer and a truck to haul it. My sweet insurance agent and friend, Teresa B. made some phone calls and before we knew it Direct Insurance had donated a trailer. And on May 22, 2012, we got Kevin's van. It took two tow trucks from Johnny's Wrecker Service and eleven people to get it on the trailer due to the fact that it couldn't be steered. But we did it! Where in the world would I store it, you might be thinking? The answer to that question would be . . . my front yard. My long time friends, Karen and Jim let us borrow their pickup truck to haul the trailer. And we were ready to go.

TOW VEHICLE

On December 19, 2012, Direct Insurance presented 1N3 with our own SUV to haul the trailer that carried Kevin's van! It was amazing to have their support of our mission.

1,629 DAYS

Everything was going well and we were on the road a lot. But there came a time when I needed something to change. Everyday when I opened my door to walk my dog the first thing I saw was Kevin's mangled van . . . every morning for 1,629 days. On November 6, 2016, I had a meltdown when I walked out and saw it. I decided I could not see it first thing one more day. So my husband moved it to the RV Park Palace, who agreed to sponsor 1N3 and store it. When that sponsorship was over, our friends at Rick's Lock and Key gave us a space to store the van and trailer.

HAVE AWARENESS WILL TRAVEL

We have taken it to schools, rehabilitation centers, a DARE conference, community events, fairs, and festivals.

SHARING OUR 1N3 STORY

On June 25, 2012, we did our first "Choices Matter" presentation at our local Haman's New Drivers in Hixson,

Tennessee. What better place to share our story than to a group of students learning to drive safely.

The word started to spread about our story and we were getting invitations to speak from everywhere. We were doing presentations every week. We have spoken at a wide variety of events. You name it, we have probably done it. The most events we did in one month was twenty-one! Over half of those were high schools in the Spring.

To date at the time this book is published, we have spoken to hundreds of audiences with hundreds of thousands in attendance. We have also shared our story at community events, to passer-by groups of people calculating in the millions! And that number continues to grow. We want to reach people from all walks of life, because drunk driving is no respecter of persons. It can impact anyone at any time.

OTHER 1N3 STORIES

The more our team was out in the community meeting people at events, or even just while we were out doing our personal life wearing a 1N3 t-shirt, the list of people we met who had also been impacted continued to grow. While it was sad to know someone else was living this same journey, it was also comforting to know we were not alone. We have had several of them to come and also speak and share their 1N3 story of how they were impacted by drunk driving. And yes, we have those who were the drunk driver speak and share how it can mess your life up as well as someone else's. The more people who stand up to share their story, no matter where it is, the more lives we can save. Who knows, the life we save may even be your own.

THEN THERE WERE TWO

We were moving right along in our presentations. We were having up to five different speakers sharing the stage telling their story. We were in a groove and everyone knew their part and how much time they had to speak. It was great!

Then the day came that I had been hoping would one day become a reality, the day that everything would change. I had daydreamed about it, discussed it with other members of the team, and prayed that I would be prepared when the day came. Latisha had been released from prison upon my request and she was joining the team! YES, we were going to stand side by side and share OUR story together in tandem, bouncing back and forth though the timeline of the events of that horrible day!

What would that look like? How would we make it work? I had been telling both sides of the story myself. But I knew adding Latisha would make a bigger impact and take our presentation to the next level. She had never spoken before, but wanted to be part of the solution even though she was nervous about how people would react. It was awkward at first and more

CHOICES

of an interview with me sharing and then asking her questions and she would answer. But we weren't sure how else to do it at the time.

Then in March 2014 on a speaking trip in Mississippi, it all changed. Our team had two adjoining rooms at our hotel. We had already done our first event that evening and everyone was hanging out between the two rooms and chatting. I was sitting on the bed trying to make some changes in our presentation on my laptop when Latisha spoke up and said, "Can we try our presentation a different way?" I was surprised but open to anything that would make it easier and flow better. I said, "Sure we can, what is your idea?"

She plopped on the bed beside me and started telling me her idea. And I pulled up a new PowerPoint and started from scratch.

Together we constructed a whole new presentation and did it the next morning at the high school. It was amazing! Today we still do our Talk the same way, and even though we have chosen not to memorize word for word what we will say, we always get our point across. We don't always tell the same details every time, sometimes we remember things that we had not remembered until that moment about what happened and we share it. Sometimes I cry and sometimes Latisha cries. When it happens we just pause and take a moment, then continue. I'm thankful we have never lost it at the same time.

To this day we still speak together. There are days when Latisha can't be at our presentations and it feels strange not having her there. It's like we are each other's support. I'm so thankful that she has chosen to make 1N3 her mission too, and stand beside me to make an impact on the world. Together we have changed so many lives with our story. I can't wait to see what is in the future for us as we continue to share our 1N3 story.

To find out more about 1N3, please visit our website, www.iam1n3.org. You can also checkout our social media on Facebook, Twitter, and Instgram @iam1N3.

CHOICES

Chapter 9

The Ripple Effect

BECAUSE MY BOOK is all about choices and how one choice to drink and drive caused a ripple effect, I have asked several people who were impacted by that one choice to share how they were impacted. That one choice had a very wide ripple effect from someone who only met Kevin once to those who knew him his whole life. The following are their own words and individual reactions to Kevin's death.

Their stories are in no particular order. And their names appear as they requested.

CHOICES

ALICIA

I met Kevin at a young age, third or fourth grade, I think, and the two of us instantly clicked. We had the same ridiculous sense of humor, the same taste in music, and both somehow loved adding milk to our ice cream. We loved the little ice crystals that formed on the top, which is such a specific interest that it could only be perceived by us as divine intervention. Nothing was better than that, except of course lounging on the couch with said ice cream while watching Jackie Chan marathons. That was another thing we had in common, our love for martial arts, especially Jackie Chan since his humor perfectly mirrored our own.

The first day I met him was actually at my own house. We were hosting some sort of social get-together, mostly with kids who were older than me, so I sat on the couch alone watching, "Rumble In the Bronx." Next thing I knew, some strange boy had plopped down next to me, confessing his love for Jackie Chan, and it was the start of a beautiful friendship. After that, we were pretty much conjoined at the hip, even to the point that his family became my second family and vice versa. Our moms became close friends, so it only seemed natural. Growing up, we always introduced each other as brother and sister.

A few years later, I experienced a little family trouble in high school. We grew apart since the only time we had together was on Sunday at church. We kept in touch a little here and there online, but it wasn't the same as seeing him in person. Then came my high school graduation. I invited him, not really expecting him to show up, but he did. That was one of the most beautiful qualities about Kevin. He was truly excited for the accomplishments of others and was *always* there to celebrate the good times. Thinking back on it now, I don't know why I was so surprised to see him show up on my doorstep. It was simply who he was. I introduced him to all of my school friends, and let me tell you, the ladies swooned. *Swooned.* He had the biggest heart and was so considerate, opening doors for my lady friends and surrendering seats for them when there wasn't enough room at the table. I, of course, already knew this about him, so his behavior didn't surprise me, but for all of my gal pals, he was like some strange alien who had landed on Earth. It became this on-running joke between us. We even had our picture taken with him: three of us girls visually swooning over his flexed muscles. To this day, it's still one of my favorite photos.

He was even there for me when I started tattooing professionally. One day, he asked me to sketch up some sort of cross/snowflake hybrid (a symbol for one of his invented comic book characters). I obeyed and came up with something that was halfway decent, but not quite right. He assured me the design was perfect, but I refused to relinquish the paper into his hands, determined to come up with something far better. He thought I couldn't do it, but I'm glad to say that I quickly proved him wrong, coming up with a design that suited him so well that he decided to have me tattoo it on his arm. Our friendship was like that. He always trusted in me, a fact that I never fully understood back then, but now that I'm older, I understand how rare that is to find. He always saw so much more in me than I could ever see in myself, except for my sketches. In his opinion, each and every one was perfect and needed no embellishments, no matter how I felt about them.

Unfortunately, we later had another span of time where we

grew apart. It wasn't like either of us wanted the space, but I had found myself in a dangerous situation, one that kept me away from friends and family. I was completely isolated. Three years passed before I realized I needed help. I reached out to Kevin when things got exponentially worse, and as always, he was there for me. I fought for my freedom and happiness, and he encouraged me every step of the way. I stayed at his place about two times a week since his house was closer to my workplace than mine. We fell back into our usual rhythm and it was as though the time without each other had never existed. I got him a job working with me and again we were figuratively conjoined at the hip until the night of the accident.

The two of us had made plans to celebrate when my freedom would officially be mine again. There was some paperwork that I was eagerly waiting on, and when it went through, my life could be whatever I wanted it to be. Kevin insisted that we celebrate, so we made plans for dinner and a movie.

The day before our plans, I was with my mom when she received the call from Tiki. Kevin had been in an accident. From the phone call, we didn't know if it was serious, but my heart dropped all the same. Somehow, I knew. We rushed to the hospital and stayed the entire day, hoping and praying for better news that didn't come. I didn't want to go home that night. It was hard to go about life as if my friend wasn't lying injured in a hospital bed.

The next day, Kevin's family provided us all with the opportunity to see him and say our goodbyes. It became clear that he could never recover from his injuries. I remember heading to the hospital that morning, fantasizing about him waking up in his hospital bed and how I could tease him for spoiling our plans, but that conversation never happened. He was simply gone.

People never prepare you for what to expect after losing a loved one. I had lost others before, but no one so important to me. Some nights I dreamt about him. I woke up in the middle of the night and got dressed, thinking that I was supposed to meet him and that I was going to be late, but then reality would sink in and I would remember that he was gone. Sometimes I thought I saw him on the street or in a restaurant. I guess my brain was just trying to fill the void. I became angry with myself and even angry with other people for not grieving a certain way. I lost interest in hobbies that used to thrill me. I didn't want to live in a world without him in it.

He passed away on the day of our scheduled celebration, which was a tough pill to swallow. On one hand, I had my freedom back, but on another I had lost someone dear to me. It didn't seem fair that such a beautiful person could be taken when he seemed as essential as sunlight. He was a source of strength and joy for many people, and now they would need to learn to be strong and happy for themselves.

I had little hope for my own future, but I had no idea that beauty could often come from tragedy.

I remembered a song that the two of us sung together in Kevin's living room. The lyrics ironically captured how we all felt about him, so I told Tiki and Derek about it. We sat listening to the song in the same exact place where Kevin and I first sang it together, and we decided to perform it at his funeral. It was one of the most difficult things I've ever done. To tell you the truth, I wasn't very happy about it at the time. I already have performance anxiety, and performing something so private made it difficult to even get the words out when the time came. I remember trying desperately not to cry on stage in front of everyone. There was this stubborn lump in my throat that wouldn't go away. Still, Derek and I managed to get through it, and sharing that moment meant a great deal to a lot of people.

I think a month passed when Derek called to ask if I would record it with him. He apparently had a friend with a studio and some recording equipment, and it was for Kevin, so I agreed. Little did I know that I would be meeting my future husband.

The three of us clicked during the recording process and we began referring to ourselves as the Three Amigos. Derek apparently saw sparks and even schemed to cancel our plans at the last minute one night in an attempt to get us alone together. Not long after, we actually began dating.

The day we married, I wore a garter that was reserved for Kevin. We had Derek wear it during the reception in Kevin's honor. It was important to my husband and me that the man who brought us together should be honored at our wedding. It hurts sometimes to know that I wouldn't have met my husband if it had not been for the death of a best friend, but at the same time I'm thankful. It's a strange and confusing feeling, but in this way, it's almost like Kevin has given his blessing.

I stated earlier that sometimes beauty can stem from tragedy. To some, it may sound strange or insensitive, but for all of us it's simply a truth that we've come to realize. My marriage wasn't the only thing to be thankful for. Kevin was an organ donor and saved lives that would have otherwise been lost. We used to love reading comics and discussing our favorite super heroes. Now Kevin is mine.

CASEY BROSTEK

I was asked to explain my part of "Kevin's Story" which I hate saying, because it seems that's all it is now, a story. Then again, I guess I'd rather refer to it as "Kevin's Story" rather than calling it what it really is, because even though a person will die, a story can live forever if told correctly.

So, who was Kevin? My best friend. My brother. Kevin was that one friend we all have who understood me when I didn't have any words to say. He was my conscience at times, my logic at others. He kept me out of trouble, or at least helped me not get caught. He was my sidekick and I was his and for the longest time, everything was awesome. And then I met a girl. I decided I wanted that girl to become a girlfriend, so that happened and eventually, I wanted that girlfriend to become a fiancé and there was no doubt in my mind who my best man was going to be.

Keep in mind, I have a couple of brothers, and one was not too happy when he found out Kevin was first pick to fill the slot. In fact, Kevin was the only one picked because I already knew that he wasn't going to pass on this kind of arrangement. So, the day finally came to turn my fiancé into a wife, and strangely, I had no last minute jitters (as the movies portray to be the norm) because I was marrying the perfect bride, and I had the best best man anyone could ask for. I'd forgotten pins; you know, to pin the lapels, or whatever. I didn't have to ask him to do a thing. He already knew what I'd forgotten to do and was already on his way to the Dollar General to pick up some pins. I didn't have to worry about a thing, and with an anxiety disorder, that was a breath of fresh air. The wedding went off without a hitch.

CHOICES

Then came our honeymoon, and of course, Kevin was delighted when I asked him to house/pet sit for a week. He packed up a bag and lived in our house while we were away. Everything was a first for me, first time on an airplane, first time in Atlanta, first time stuck overnight at the Atlanta airport, first time out of the United States. My wife and I were in St. Lucia for our honeymoon, and it was the most beautiful place I'd ever seen. Three days into our exotic island paradise and another first experience came, a Facebook message that read something along the lines of "Call me. It's an emergency" from a friend named Kris. Luckily, the house we were staying in had Wifi, which I assume is incredibly rare there, so I received the message almost instantly. I called Big K up and his first words to me were, "-sigh- Man, Kevin had an accident." Now, I've gotten this call before, you know--fender benders with friends and family, so I was slightly amused when I asked, "Oh sh-t. Is he okay?" I had a slight chuckle. It stopped pretty quickly when I heard my friend on the other end say, "No." He was crying. This is a big guy, hence the nickname, Big K. He's not supposed to be crying. I don't remember what I asked after that, or what he said. I remember not feeling anything, no thoughts, no anything and we ended the call. I remember staring blankly to the floor for a while as my new wife asked if I was okay. And I remember that I literally could not breathe. I was hyperventilating. I don't even think I had time for an anxiety attack before I started crying, and then I had to explain to my wife why I was crying, and then she was crying. Kevin was not dead yet. He was in a hospital, but it was not looking good. I found the strength to stop crying long enough to call his mom. I called Big K. I called everybody I could think of to keep me updated, which they did, for a while. Then, I stopped getting updated. I knew something was about to happen because Kevin's family wasn't saying much of anything to anyone. But I had to know. I didn't have time to be left out of the loop. This was my best friend, so I called his brother--a lot. Derek gave me more details, even though I'm fairly certain he was supposed to keep it quiet, and for that, I love him.

The rest of the honeymoon was surreal. It was still amazing, but we didn't have any fun. We still had a lot of firsts but they meant nothing. We tried to catch a flight home, but the airport wouldn't allow us. Then, Kevin's brain swelled. There was no activity and it was time to let him go. I begged for them to wait one more day so that I could come home and say goodbye. There was no way. The next morning, we were driving back to the village from a volcano, or a forest, I don't remember. As I sat in that 'taxi' looking out of the window, I saw a rainbow and I cried again because I felt it; I felt at that exact moment, Kevin was gone. Now, I don't believe in garbage like that, even today. But I believe that it happened on that day, because as soon as we got back, I received the message that they let Kevin go.

I had hope until that very moment that Kevin would pull through. I can't say he was strong, because he kind of wasn't. In fact, he was kind of a baby when it came to getting sick. But I was so afraid of losing him that I convinced myself it wasn't going to happen. It did, though. As soon as I saw that message, I fell into a VERY dark place. So, here's a bit about me: if I want something, I get it, and I'm good at getting it. And what I wanted was the name of the woman who killed him. I wanted to know her address. I wanted to know how many kids she had and what kind of car she drives and where she works. I knew every detail of that woman in a matter of hours. I found her Facebook. Hell, I could probably tell you the last update if it wasn't so long ago. I was not myself and honestly, I have no idea what I was going to do with that information, but I had it in case I needed it. And at this point, I no longer had a best friend to talk me out of whatever may have popped into my mind.

It was the day to come home, and we were on that plane in a hurry. I needed to be home. I didn't think about my wife, I didn't think about my honeymoon forever being associated with the death of my best friend, and I didn't think about the fact that my pets were not being taken care of (it turns out, they were thanks to my other family that broke into our apartment for us). I could not think of anything. I could not feel anything. I had a place to be, and I had to be there. Sadly, that place was a funeral.

If you ask me what the most impacting moment was, I would have to say it is when I was talking to our friend Roderick and how I was apologizing I was not there to say goodbye, and Roderick's words will never EVER leave me. He said to me, "You didn't want to be there, man." The look on his face haunts me. As I write this, I'm tearing up, because at that moment, I knew. As hard as I fought to get home and to be inside the loop, Roderick was absolutely right. I didn't want to be there. I didn't want to see him like that and I didn't want to have to be attending his funeral. I stood in line to see him. It wasn't supposed to be an open casket, but they did such a good job on him that his family allowed it. Another ghostly memory was seeing him there in that casket. He didn't look like himself; no, he wasn't himself. That was not my friend. But still, I slipped the garter belt in his hands (that's a whole other story). I owed him that. I gave a speech, and it probably didn't make a damn bit of sense. I prepared something to say, but I don't prepare things, so like usual, I winged it. I don't remember a word of it, except something about Call of Duty and having each others' back. There's a video of it somewhere, but I haven't watched it. I can't. I can't relive that moment. I can't feel that way again. I remember meeting a bunch of people, and I hated them. People I didn't know... I hated them, because I didn't know them. I stood there with a smile, politely greeting them, but without knowing them, I hated them because there was no way they could have felt as strongly for Kevin as we did, his real friends. I know now, that was stupid, and I apologize to all of them here.

There was music; the whole funeral was set like a party. Everyone was standing and hugging and talking, and I looked into Q's eyes, another big ol' guy I've never even seen close to crying, and I knew what I had to do. I hugged him. In our circle, we didn't hug. Kevin was our emotional hugger type. But I hugged Q and we both cried. Runce joined in. Then Rod .Then Big K and Dick, then all of us. I can't even recall who was in that huddle anymore. But then something happened. We were crying; but no, that wasn't who we were. Kevin wouldn't want a bunch of man-babies crying over him. So, I did what any of us would have done, I made fun of Q's big ol' crying self. I made him laugh. So then I laughed. And then someone said something else and we all laughed. We were crying, but we were laughing. I wouldn't give Death the satisfaction of seeing us cry. I vowed to do what Kevin would have done. I wanted to be there for my friends and they wanted to be there for me, and if he exists, God knows I needed them to be.

I carried him to his grave; we all did. He wasn't heavy; the casket wasn't anything too much to worry about. Four of us probably could have done it easily, but we all had a hand on his box. All of his best friends were carrying him to the afterlife, sticking by him until the very end, because he would have been there for us if the tables were turned. We put him in the ground and I watched his mother drop a white rose on top of the casket. Then his brother, Derek, took a handful of dirt and dropped it in the hole. Then Mark, his Daddy did the same. It was my turn, and I grabbed a handful of dirt, but I was stopped. Mark said to me, "Please, just the family." I was lost again, lost in Hell for just a fraction of a second. I was about to explain not so politely how I was more family to that boy than he was, but I pulled myself back to reality. I wouldn't make a scene, not here. Not now. Mark didn't permit me a handful of dirt, but as I said earlier, I get what I want. I came back later that day and took my share. Again, I have to apologize for my feelings, this time to Mark. You were nothing to me that day, and for a long time after, but that's ridiculous to hold on to.

So, where are we now-a-days? Well, as many married couples do, we had a baby. We named her Ryver Frost Brostek, because Ryver Kevin Brostek sounds absurd for a little girl. Also, Ryver Frost would be an awesome super hero name if she ever decides to fight crime. We bought a house. I have a decent paying job. But here's the kicker; all of these years later and all of these great things I have, but I still have a part of me that feels empty. I still don't have a best friend. I've tried to 'promote' some of the guys in our circle, but really, after Kevin died, it seems we all grew apart. It could just be life: growing up, being too busy, but I really do feel that a lot of it has to do with the pain of losing one of our best friends--the one that was obviously the center of the group. Some of us still keep in touch, text, and Facebook and whatnot. But there's a few I haven't seen nor heard from since that day, with a few exceptions here and there. I don't know why. I'm sure I could try harder, but I just can't. I can show up out of the blue and say hey. I do that once in a while, but it will never go back to the way it was.

Kevin and I had so many plans for the future. We wanted to open a business together. I was trying to get him back in school. He wanted a business degree to further our plans. I was working towards a science degree myself. I was going to be the best man at his wedding. Our children were going to get married so that we'd officially be related. We were going to keep our couches open for the other for when 'the wife is being intolerable', which of course meant we did something wrong. And then after we grew old and eventually died, we were going to haunt people while our ghost-wives did ghost-wife things, because, you know, ghost wives don't like haunting, I guess. That part can still happen.

It was all stolen from me. That future was taken away because of Latisha Stephens, the woman who killed my best friend. It's like swallowing daggers when I hear her name; even worse when I attempt to say it. I think I've said it three times since Kevin's burial. I need to forgive her, that's what I've been told. Forgiveness is the path. But I don't know forgiveness--not for this. Forgiveness is a foreign concept for me. I WANT to forgive her, but that doesn't make sense to me. You don't forgive murderers, you hate them. You mentally rip them apart every time you remember your friend because there will never be a new memory, a new experience. I'm urged every so often by a friend to meet her. I'm told that meeting her may be that step I need to forgive, but I won't. She doesn't deserve my forgiveness. She gets plenty of that from the good people, the people like Kevin's family, and the people she is helping by retelling her stories in schools and prisons. Not from me. I am not a good person, not all the time.

I am afraid. I am absolutely terrified that if I see her, I may find myself in that same darkness. I don't know how I will react, or what I will say, or what I will do. Most likely, I will smile and say, "How's it going?" and go about my life. After all, that is the proper thing to do. But when you are that completely lost, who knows? I won't attack her, I'm not that kind of person, I'm so very certain of that, but it doesn't take a whole lot to completely ruin somebody's life. All it can take is a few words. Sometimes all it takes is a look. I don't even know if I'd recognize her at all.

This all is starting to seem really weird to me. I don't know if what I'm writing even makes sense. I'm not sure whether or not typing any of it can get me into trouble. I mean, I'm not planning to do anything. I'm just going about my life, raising my daughter and keeping the missus happy. Me? I'm completely broken on the inside, I have been for years now, but I've managed to keep it in check. I'm still happy. I still have hobbies and love spending time with my wife. I still enjoy life and watching Ryver grow up even though I know she'll never meet my best friend and he never got to meet her. I know life goes on for everyone and sometimes things happen that you can't control. That's just the way it is. If you ask me, "Do I think I'll ever find a way to let go of the anger or the sadness?" my answer is "no." I will say it without explanation. Can I still function and enjoy the rest of my time on this planet? Of course.

Tiki asked me to keep it short, so I guess this is my final apology of the night. I tried my best, but I dwindled it down as much as I could. I didn't mention anything about how we became best friends or how we worked together or how we actually WEREN'T best friends for a year or how that is still the single biggest regret of my life that I would let a petty argument waste an entire year of our friendship. I didn't mention any of our inside jokes like "I'm a worm," or, "Grow Back to Human ray". I didn't mention our talks of philosophy or getting each other through the rough times or any of the typical young adult garbage like the "You're dating my ex" kind of stuff. There's nothing here about how I wrote him into my own book or how we planned to make a video game or the (literally) countless hours of gaming and D&D type role playing we would all do. It'd take an entire book to write "Kevin's Story" from my perspective. Hopefully, you'll all be satisfied with a few pages. Kevin was a great guy, a great man, and a great person, and for all of you that never got to meet him, you really missed out.

CHOICES

CASSIE NOEL

The following is a letter I received in the mail on Wednesday, August 17, 2011, from someone I did not know. It made me so proud to be Kevin's mom that we contacted her and ask if we could share it with everyone.

How I met Kevin

Dear Tiki,

Hello! Unfortunately, the only time I've met you was at Kevin's funeral, but I did get to meet Kevin a little over a month ago. I wanted you to know the story of how I met Kevin.

My fiancé, Nick Stone, is best friends with Kris Davis, who you know was best friends with Kevin. Well a month ago, Kris called Nick and me to invite us to dinner. When we arrived at Asian Buffet on Lee Hwy., Kevin was there. I remember the first time I saw him, he reminded me of my old friends from high school. He was wearing a pinstriped hat, long hair with a Kingdom Hearts shirt and black pants. Nick already knew Kevin through Kris, and apparently they all hung out during high school.

Immediately, I liked Kevin. He was so funny and had manners (something that's rare nowadays). All through dinner, I asked Kevin all kinds of questions, just to see if I could get him to answer. To my surprise, he answered all them with ease. All through dinner, all four of us were having a great time. At the end of dinner, Kevin invited us back to his (your) house. I knew Nick was tired that night, but I wanted to learn more about Kevin, so we said yes.

We got to Kevin's house around 7:00 p.m. We hung out in the living room, the guys started to catch up and talk about video games- while I sat back and listened. I was so impressed with the openness that Kevin had. I had never met anyone like him before. While we were there, Kevin's phone rang, and the ring tone was the fairy voice from Zelda. Nick and I thought it was so cool that we had Kevin message us the sound. From that night on, that ring tone was Nick's and my ring tone. By 10:00 p.m., I was tired so Nick and I decided to head home. Before we left, we asked Kevin if he wanted to come to our upcoming wedding in September. He agreed, so we got his address. As we left, Kevin stood in the door waving goodbye. I had no idea that would be the last time I would see him.

    I sent Kevin an invitation to my wedding, but hadn't received his RSVP card back. On July 28th, I decided to text him. He texted back right away saying that yes, he would be attending. He had already taken the day off work and was excited to go. I told him that I was happy too, and that we should all get together again. He agreed and told me that he was always off on Mondays. I told him I'd get with Nick and see when we could all get together for dinner again. That was the last time I talked to him.

    I wanted to write you this letter to let you know that Kevin inspired/inspires me. From the moment I met him, I knew he was different and I loved it! Even though I only got to spend time with him once, he changed my life. He taught me to enjoy my life and approach people with open arms. That's what he did that night we met. I only wish we had more time to become better friends. I really feel like we would have been close in time. I thank God every day that I got to meet Kevin before he was killed. I think of him every day and say a prayer. I had a Batman decal with his initials above it made for my car. I put it

CHOICES

next to my driver's side window so every time I get in my car, I will think of Kevin. And the Zelda ring tone is still my ring tone; I smile every time I hear it.

I am deeply sorry for your loss and I pray God helps you find the strength to heal. Kevin touched so many people, and will never be forgotten. You are never alone in your pain, so don't forget to reach out to your loved ones. It was your strength that got me through Kevin's funeral, so thank you. May God bless you and your family in your time of need.

I hope this story helps you know that Kevin is loved by so many.

CRYSTAL, Kevin's Aunt

Dear Kevin,

The last five years has been like living in a nightmare from which I can't wake up. Some days, it seems as if you are still here and we haven't spoken for a few days, but others, I feel like I relive July 31, 2011, and August 1, 2011, down to every detail.

I am ashamed to admit the person I became after your funeral. I look back and I know I can understand what a person means when they say "temporary insanity". Can you believe I wanted to kill Latisha? Like I said, I am ashamed of that, and have come a long way since those early days; but more on that later.

There were moments at the hospital I felt like I was on auto-pilot; just going through the motions, saying things that were expected of me, but keeping how I really felt deep inside because I was scared. The TICU room is scary. Seeing you unresponsive, your hair matted with your blood, broken bones-- it was just overwhelming. I pray you heard me talking to you. Could you feel me holding your hand? Did you feel the warmth of my kiss on your forehead? Did you hear the whisper in your ear that you were not alone? My heart wants to, no, must, believe you did.

I started taking depression medication. I was sleeping most of the day, staying awake at night or crying myself to sleep. I didn't want to engage in life. I would look at my phone and want to call you. Remember our breakfasts? Eating cereal would make me collapse onto the kitchen floor and cry until there was nothing left in me.

I don't understand how our world got turned so upside

down in just an instant. I kept asking why our family? Why you? I begged God to let me take your place. I was so angry with God! So many drunks on the road, drug addicts, gang members; and God lets this happen to you? I had so many unanswered questions.

Christmases, Thanksgiving, Easter, birthdays, every day, has changed without your laughter. We tried to play Pictionary without you that first year –it didn't go well. I've retired the game from our holiday/family get togethers. Your smile and hugs can never be replaced. It took me *over a year* to remember when we last saw each other and what we said! God, I hated that feeling! It was one of desperation to find a memory I knew was there but "lost".

I had to forgive her, Kevin. Are you mad at me for that? The heart can only handle so much before it explodes and felt like I was on that path of self-destruction. Once I forgave her, again I had mixed emotions. Relief from the tightness of anger and guilt, but wondering how you would feel about that.

Then I remembered that our last visit was at Dustin's *(Crystal's son)*. Tiffany *(Dustin's wife)* had just taken pictures of you with her new camera and you two were looking over them. I stood behind you running my fingers through your hair and you did the usual and asked me not to stop. I sure miss doing that! As I was leaving, you hugged me tight and I hugged you back. We told each other "love you, see you later". It still hurts to know that later didn't come. But to have that beautiful memory every time I sit on Dustin's front porch, is priceless.

Forgiving Latisha allowed me to grow as a person. I found out hatred isn't worth it. It doesn't change anything. You can't go back in time and un-do wrongs. I quit being mad at God.

Bad things happen to good people all the time and even though I don't understand "why", I had to accept reality.

I know you are in a better place and I have to be envious of that! I wonder what your mansion looks like. Have you been to the crystal river and how bright are the streets of gold? Have you hung out with your grandmothers? What a reunion that must have been!

The memories I have are bittersweet. Happy and sad depending on the day. Going to different venues to present the story of the impact of drinking and driving has been therapeutic for me. Sometimes I can't make it through a speech without crying and others, I'm fine. That's okay. Crying is healing.

A part of you still lives on through others. Organ donation was something I knew about but had no experience with until your wreck. I wasn't sure how to act or what to feel when we met Melvin. You would love him though! He and his family are so loving and laugh all the time! His hugs aren't yours, but they sure come close.

I found out, life goes on, Kevin. I've lost loved ones before but not in the traumatic way we lost you. That was an experience I wouldn't wish on my worst enemy. The family still gets together, we still love, we still laugh. We still cry. I believe we always will. I see Batman symbols everywhere and think of you with a smile. I eat "our" cereal and think of you. I don't go to your grave as often as I did; I can't. It keeps me in a place of sadness and hurt, so I remember you in my way--in the little things that make me smile, in the ways that make me go on.

Until we are together again, "love you, see you later".

Forever your "favorite Aunt",

I love you Kev.

CHOICES

DIXIE RENE' BELL, Kevin's Mimi

July 31, 2011, was one of the worst days of my life. It was Sunday morning and my husband Charlie and I were getting ready for church. My son-in-law, Tom, called to tell me that I needed to get to the hospital as quickly as possible because my grandson, Kevin, had been in a bad car wreck. Immediately Charlie and I drove to the hospital. Kevin was in surgery. Family and friends started arriving. We had no idea how serious this wreck had been. From surgery, they took Kevin to the trauma unit where they let us all go in to see him. I was not prepared for what I was about to see. Kevin was in a coma and on a ventilator. The left side of his head was bloody and badly bruised. Almost every bone in his body was broken. All I could do was pray and cry, just hoping Kevin would wake up and be okay. But there was no movement, no sign of life. The machine was breathing for him. All I wanted to do was hold and kiss his sweet face, but all I could do was rub his hands and pray in the Spirit for him.

We went back to the family room and the doctor came in. The news he gave us was not good. Kevin's brain was swelling and they couldn't stop it, but we kept going in to see him and praying. What now seem like days was approximately 31 hours when the doctor came in and told us that we needed to make a decision because Kevin was brain dead. I wanted to scream, "Noooo! We can't let him go!!!" But we only had a few hours to make that decision. That is the hardest decision anyone could ever have to make. To say, this is the end, it's over, and let him go. The only way my daughter, Tiki, had the strength to make that decision was by the grace of God. How do you tell someone that you love so much, good-bye? How? To know on this earth, we'll never see him again, never hear his voice, or feel his touch, or put your arms around him again. It's the most smothering feeling I know. I wanted to run and scream, "STOP!" He was 25 years old, but was my grandbaby, and there was Tiki, my baby girl, watching her baby die. There was Derek, Kevin's brother, watching his baby brother die. They had always been best friends. His cousin, Dustin. They had been like brothers. The three of them had been the Ninja Turtles together. I was hurting, my heart was breaking, but I wanted to stop the hurt and pain for them. I'd always been able to help them when they were hurting before, but this time I couldn't. I couldn't stop the pain for me and I couldn't stop it for them, no matter how badly I wanted to. I prayed for comfort and I know the sweet Holy Spirit comforted us. That's the only way we got through the next few days. The decision to donate Kevin's organs was also made because we knew that was what Kevin wanted. His friend, Blake, had passed away a couple of years before and was an organ donor. Kevin told his Mom that, because he was an organ donor, Blake was a Super hero, and that if anything ever happened to him he wanted to be an organ donor, a Super hero. Kevin was such a giver and he is my Super hero.

So now there is the autopsy, and we were having to wait for days until they finished the autopsy for Kevin's organs to be harvested. We didn't even know what day to plan his funeral. The waiting was awful; knowing they were taking parts of his body was hard, but it gave us time to plan his funeral, or as we called it, Kevin's Home Going Party, the Celebration of His Life that was way too short. We planned a party that Kevin would have wanted if he had planned it himself.

CHOICES

There were sleepless nights, and crying all night long. I still had to work, so I cried and worked until finally it was time for his service. So many friends and family came to honor him. I've never been more proud of my family. Tiki and Tom spoke about what a great son Kevin was and funny stories about him. Derek sang, "Your Guardian Angel", with Kevin's best friend, Alicia. Every word that was spoken about him and every song that was sung was so much Kevin. Michael Ketterer sang, "You're Beautiful", and a song that he wrote called, "Dusty Road", was awesome! They are on YouTube if you want to listen to them. We had all of Kevin's favorite things there. Batman, Marvel Comics, Ninja Turtles, his bowling ball, and his trumpet. We celebrated his life with everything we had in us. Kevin would have loved it! Then his home going service was over, and now there is life without Kevin. I had such an empty feeling. There was a hole in my heart that only he could fill. My broken heart and mind were filled with sweet memories. Only a few days before Kevin had called me to ask me if I was going to the hospital to visit his grandfather, Theo, his Pipi. Kevin was going to visit him and he had a new girlfriend with him and he wanted me to meet her. I had just left the hospital and was almost home. I said, "Oh Baby, I just left there. I wish I had known you were coming and I would have stayed." I was taking care of my Daddy and needed to make supper, but everything inside me wanted to turn around and go back to the hospital. Oh how I wish I had gone back for just one more hug. Kevin said, "That's ok, Mimi. I just didn't want you to be left out." We talked for a few more minutes and I said, "I love you so much, Kevin!" He said, "I love you too, Mimi. Sameristicaler!" And we laughed. It was a word that he had made up for "just us" when we said good-bye on the phone or were together. "I love you Mimi. Sameristicaler!" It was "our love word". Now he was 25 and hadn't said it in a while until that night. That would be the last time I would ever hear him say that to me. I will cherish those few minutes for the rest of my life. Now all I have are memories and I live for those sweet memories to show up. I talk about them and laugh and cry. I do whatever I must to keep them alive. I wasn't finished, Kevin. I wasn't finished making memories with you! I wasn't done making you banana pudding for your birthdays. I wasn't done making deviled eggs, and baked beans, and things you loved so much for Thanksgiving and Christmas. I'm still not done. I miss you so much Kevin!

It's been over seven years now since you left us. It's still fresh in my heart. There are days it feels like it just happened. Only God and prayer get me through it. Talking with Tiki and reminiscing. I have the sweetest assurance that I know where Kevin is. One of my favorite memories is Kevin coming to church a few months before he died. He sat on the front seat on the front row with Tiki and Tom. As soon as the alter call was given Kevin stepped forward. We all went down to pray with him. When it was over I said, "I'm so proud of you, Kevin." and he said, "I just got tired of trying to do it by myself."

Kevin is in Heaven! He's in my future because Heaven IS for Real. Jesus made it possible. Kevin said, "I made it! It's amazing! I didn't know it was going to be like this!" I believe it with all my heart and am in great anticipation for that reunion day! I know Kevin is waiting there with our other loved ones, with those long arms opened wide. I can hardly wait for his sweet hugs.

Sameristicaler, Kevin! I love you baby! See you soon!

CHOICES

TALISA WALKER

August 1, 2011, will forever be forged in my memory and my heart. It's the day I lost my person, my soul mate. He was taken from me, because someone decided to drink and drive.

We only knew each other for a short time, but in that short time we just had an unspoken love. The way he looked at me and smiled just warmed my heart. Even though we never said the words out loud I know he loved me, and I believe he knew I loved him too.

Our first date started out as any typical date would, we went out to eat. We met up at Ichiban and as soon as I walked the door the first thing I noticed was his big smile. The smile I later learned was his famous sunshine smile that he wore so proudly. I also noticed his fedora hat he was rocking. We were seated by ourselves, because it was close to closing time. I loved that we were by ourselves. It gave us time to really focus on one another and get to know each other. It was so easy to talk to him and I loved that he was so eager to learn about me just as I was him. Neither one of us even ate that much, because we were too busy learning about one another. We got so lost in each other that we lost track of time and soon we realized that they were closing. He walked me out to my car and once again we stood there just talking away.

It still amazes me to this day the connection we shared and the way he made me feel that night. He then asked if I'd like to accompany him to his house to meet a couple of his friends. Once we got to the house we all just sat and talked for a while getting to know one another. We then decided to watch Toy Story 3. I'll never forget the joy on Kevin's face while watching that movie. We laughed through the entire movie.

As I was sitting there, I leaned on him a little bit with my hands in my lap and he ever so slightly started moving his hand towards mine then finally he grabbed my hand and all I could do was smile. It was so cute how timid he was. Then his friend, Ali (Alicia), started playing this song on the ukulele and they were singing. It was such a beautiful song. It quickly became a favorite song of mine. By the time I left it was 5:00 a.m. He walked me to my car gave me a hug and told me to text him when I got home. Right before I went to pull away, he asked me to be his girlfriend and I just knew right away that it was a big yes. I just had a feeling it was the start of something great.

One day when Kevin was at my house he saw that I had window markers. So he took a few of them and started drawing a batman symbol on my window. Batman was his favorite superhero. As he drew it he told me that he was putting it there so I knew that no matter what happened he was always going to be there for me watching over me. Neither of us knew that a few short days after this he would be gone forever, but I know that he's forever watching over me.

Kevin's last day is one I'll always treasure. We met my parents at the boat dock to spend the day out on the water. It was the first time in a long time he had been on a boat and the first time he had been tubing behind a boat. It was such a great time. I loved seeing his big smile while he was riding the tube. He was so happy that day. That is exactly how I will always remember him; smiling on that intertube. He had to go to work later that day so we dropped him off at the dock. I never would have thought in a million years that it would be the last time I would ever see his smiling face, or even hear his voice. When he got off work I got a text from him letting me know that he would call me when he got home, a call that never came.

July 31 2011, I woke up with a horrible feeling. I just knew something was wrong. I went and grabbed my phone and it was filled with so many notifications. Kevin had been in a wreck and was in the ICU. I was at my parent's house so I rushed into their room and told them I needed to leave immediately. I rushed to the hospital and was greeted by his family. His mom took me into a big hug. I was told that he was hit by someone who chose to drink and drive. It made me angry knowing that it could have been avoided. I stayed sitting there in the waiting room almost all day with his family. Just hoping and praying for the best.

August 1, 2011, the horrible news came. There was too much swelling on Kevin's brain and he was brain dead. His family had made the decision for him to donate his organs; a decision that everyone knew he would want. He loved super heroes, and donating his organs meant he could be a superhero and save lives. But before this, his family let us all go in and say goodbye to him. It was one of the hardest things I've ever had to do. I wasn't sure I'd be able to do it at first, but I'm glad I did. I walked into the room held his hand knowing it'd be the last time.

The following weeks, even months after he was gone I had a hard time dealing. I was mad, angry, and sad. I didn't understand why he had been taken from me, especially when I knew that if the woman who hit him hadn't of been drinking, it probably never would have happened. I stayed angry for a good while. I wasn't ready to forgive or let go. A year later I got to meet Melvin, the guy who received Kevin's heart; it was a really touching moment for me. I got to hear Kevin's heart beat again and it was a wonderful feeling. Seeing the good that came out of a tragedy made it easier to let go.

When I first heard that his family had asked for Latisha, the woman who hit him, to be released early I was angry. I didn't understand how they could be so forgiving. I was still upset, and angry that she had taken him from me. Then I met her and she came up to me gave me a hug and told me how sorry she was for everything and I could tell that she really meant it. It was a great feeling to finally forgive her so I could let go of all the anger I had been carrying around.

It's been seven years now and I still think about Kevin. I see something Batman and it reminds me of him. I still miss him and his smile. I still feel the pain of losing someone so suddenly. It's just a pain that doesn't ever fully go away. All of this could have been avoided if someone had not gotten behind the wheel drinking. I hope that this story might make other people realize that their actions not only hurt themselves, but others too. Drinking and driving is something no one should do. Drinking and driving can alter someone's entire life, like mine. I don't want anyone to have to go through what I have been through. It's such a hard thing to deal with. Every day I have to live without him because he was taken from me.

After I lost Kevin, I was lost. I didn't think I'd find a love like his again. I went searching in the wrong places for it, married the wrong guy thinking I'd found it. I am now remarried and I have found someone who loves me like Kevin did and I can't help but think that it is how Kevin is watching over me.

Kevin is and was the best person I've ever met. He always had a smile on his face and he was always so positive. My time with him taught me a lot and I will always treasure the time we had together. When Kevin moved to Heaven, we lost such a wonderful soul. He is my super hero, always watching over me like he said he would.

LATISHA STEPHENS

My name is Latisha Stephens. Most of you probably know by what you've read so far that I was the drunk driver that will always be responsible for Kevin's death. There is also more to me than the drunk driver that I once was.

Prior to July 31, 2011, I was a single mom of two boys, eleven and thirteen, trying to make ends meet like the average person. I had an eleven year career at a local hospital. My bills were paid. I provided a home for my boys and they had everything they needed. I had lots of "friends" and family that I spent time with. They were always there to help me with my children, as being a single mom can be challenging. When my children were home I was with them, but when they were spending time elsewhere, I would go out with my "friends". I thought I deserved to enjoy myself and get out with my friends when my boys weren't with me. I worked hard and provided for my family so having a little fun never hurt anyone, right? Wrong. I suppose if you are a responsible person and consider everyone's safety, if you decide to intoxicate yourself, then it probably would be ok. I unfortunately did not do just that. I honestly didn't think anything like this would ever happen to me. It's sad but it never crossed my mind that I could hurt an innocent person. At the most I thought that I may get a DUI, get arrested. I never thought that I may kill someone! I'm not sure what went wrong in my life for me not to consider this, but I will strive to make it my life mission to be sure others know the dangers of drinking and driving. You see, I had never known anyone that this has happened to, nor had anyone ever talked to me about it. Of course, I have seen it on the news or in movies, but for it to happen to me was unthinkable. Most people think

CHOICES

nothing like this can happen to them, BUT it can! It most definitely will happen if bad choices are continuously made time and time again! It eventually catches up with you. I am living proof of that.

It was the weekend and my co-worker was having a housewarming party after the purchase of her first home. I picked up a friend on the way to the party. We had just planned to go to the party for a while and then go home. It didn't occur to us about how we were getting home. We thought we would just have a couple of drinks, hang out for a while, and that would be all. When drinking alcohol, plans tend to change. After visiting with our friends and being there for several hours, we decided to go out and meet some other friends at a bar. We had been drinking alcohol at the party and shouldn't have been driving, but did it anyway. Apparently I had more than I thought, because I don't recall anything shortly after arriving at the bar. It was later told to me by my friend that was with me, who was also intoxicated, what she remembered.

I tried to drive her home, but we didn't make it very far before she had me pull over. She was scared we weren't going to make it to her house safely. We had some people following us and one of them (also intoxicated) drove us the rest of the way. They tried to get me to stay, but I was stubborn and was determined to drive home. (I don't put any of the blame on them. It was my choice to drink and drive. I take 100% responsibility for my actions.) The jeep had been left in the street with the keys in the ignition. I climbed into the driver's seat from the back seat and drove away. I got on the highway going north in a southbound lane and drove over four miles, crossed a bridge, and then hit Kevin head on. I was admitted to the hospital with several injuries that turned out to be life threatening, and at the time I had no idea that I had killed someone. I found out later that my blood alcohol level was 0.235 at the time of the wreck, three times the legal limit! That alone was enough to kill me. What I do remember was waking up at the hospital in pain and angry that I was there. I knew that I had made a huge mistake, and at that time I thought I could fix it. Little did I know that there wasn't anything in this world I could do to make this situation ok. After I was stable my parents had to break the news to me. The unimaginable had happened. I had killed someone and had to face it and take responsibility.

    I could go into detail about how hard life has been on me and the multiple situations I had survived. As far back as birth, it was just one thing after another. Far more than one person should have to endure. But I will not put you through all of that. Over the years, I have learned to live with it the best way I know how. In a away, I do think my past had an impact on how I turned out. But that is no excuse for this situation. I take full responsibility for the heartache I have caused countless amounts of people. (Knowing every day that I am the reason Kevin is not here on this earth enjoying every day life with his loved ones as he should be.) It's a simple little things that remind me daily. Like watching a TV show with my son, out of nowhere it'll hit me that Kevin will never be able to do that. I just have to walk away and cry sometimes. Pray about it. Sometimes I even talk to Kevin himself. It is something that I alone will have to deal with for the rest of my life. I have put a life sentence on them as well. I can't change that. I can give it to God and pray for them. I can change my lifestyle and purpose. I can be a better mother, wife, friend, and person in general. I can hold my head high and live my life as God wants me to knowing that I have been forgiven. That God and I have already dealt with my sin and he is truly the only one I will allow to hold it over my head, and He won't. I can and will make a difference. I will do what I can to see that this doesn't happen to other people. I will never forget what I have done, but by the grace of God I am still here, and I will be the person He intended for me to be. I am also very grateful for the forgiveness and love I have been shown by Tiki and her family. I love Tiki in a way I cannot describe. It is truly a love I have never felt before. I have a tremendous amount of love and respect for her. I have learned so much from her forgiveness. It has allowed me to forgive people in my past, and I'm sure future, that otherwise I would not have allowed to happen. It has opened up so many doors for me that I am very thankful for. The outcome of this tragedy could have been so different. I am forever grateful for her love and forgiveness. I am a better person with the love she has shown me and the help from my Lord and Savior.

I hope this chapter has shown you the impact of just one choice. There were so many people who were impacted by this one choice. The ripples are so far reaching they cannot be counted. Your choices matter!

Chapter 10

COMING OUT OF THE FOG

THEN AND NOW

WRITING THIS BOOK has been a seven-year journey that started in 2012. Time and again, I set deadlines that I failed to meet. I finally decided to go with God's timing and not mine. Then I realized that the things I was writing in that moment were things that I remembered about that point in time that were hidden by the fog of grief. Little by little the fog has lifted and God has brought those times to my mind and showed me where He had been there working behind the scenes. Then I would see where those moments made me a better version of myself. I am so grateful to know God and that this journey has brought me closer to Him.

DAY 3,007

So here I am on day 3,007 of my journey without Kevin, writing my last chapter. I just now realized that with this being the seventh year of writing that seven is the number of completion. How fitting to be finishing now, because the number eight represents a new beginning. When this book is completed it will be a new beginning for me, one for which I am so ready!

Thinking back over this journey to the person I was in July 2011 to the person I am now in October 2019, it is hard to explain the person I see today.

I am the same, but also very much different than who I recognize when I look in the mirror. Yet, I see a new, and real me.

THE DARKROOM

This horrific life-altering event has been the hardest thing I have ever encountered. I pray I will never go through anything harder. It has also molded me into the woman I am today. I was locked in a very dark room for a long time and couldn't find my way out. And just like God, He opened my eyes to see that a negative must be developed in the dark. If it is exposed to the light before it has developed, the beautiful photograph will be ruined. But if the negative goes through the proper developing process, there is a waiting time for the full beauty of the photograph to be seen.

This is what God was doing in that darkroom. He was developing the horrible negative life-altering event in time where I wanted to lay on Kevin's grave and die too. What has emerged is a beautiful picture of forgiveness that reflects His unconditional love and forgiveness. This is a free gift for all of mankind that cost Him everything. There were many times along the way where I thought I was ready to come out of that darkroom. I could have messed up the image, but I'm so glad I chose to be patient and wait. Because He finally opened the door and the light is so brilliant and bright and the picture He developed is better than anything I would have ever dreamed.

Before Kevin left this earth I thought I knew exactly what my purpose was and where my life was headed. In some ways it is the same, but today it is much more defined with a broader reach. I'm thankful for all the opportunities that I have had, and will have in the future, to share Kevin's story and mine. It has been part of the healing process and will continue to be.

However, to say, "I am over it", "past it", "back to normal", "moved on", or any other phrase like that, I will never be any of those things. As I said in previous chapters, I wanted to die and could not see life because of the mental and emotional fog. While I do not mourn Kevin any longer, there will always be times that I feel the grief of not having Kevin here. I don't live in a state of grief or let it control me. But I do allow myself to feel what I need to feel and walk through that moment holding God's hand. I do miss Kevin more than words can explain, because he is forever a part of me. But my hope is in the fact that Kevin is not just in my past, he is in my future waiting for me! Until then I choose to wake up thankful for the day and say, "Yes", to whatever God's plan is for that day. I keep my eyes and heart open to touch someone's life that needs encouragement and hope that there is a place of joy in this life after tragedy. For me, forgiveness has been the vehicle to bring me to that place.

There will never be "the end" to this story. There will always be more I could add. So, I hope that this book has encouraged you in some way and brought hope. If you have read this book to the end and still say to yourself, "I don't see how she did it," I want to encourage you to choose to start somewhere trusting God to work in your life. If you are mourning or grieving over a loved one, choose to ask God to walk you through your valley, and to carry you on the days you can't find the strength to walk. If you have been hurt by someone, choose to forgive. If you have hurt someone, choose to ask for forgiveness.

If you do not have a relationship with God and want to know and feel the peace and joy that I have, what are you waiting for? Choose to not allow Satan to rob anymore of your life from you. You can say the following prayer and start an amazing adventure with Jesus now.

"God, thank You for loving me just as I am in this moment. You love me no matter what I have or haven't done. I could never earn your love, because You have given it freely and unconditionally. Thank you for sending Your Son, Jesus, to die in my place, to pay the price for my sin and provide forgiveness. I ask for Your forgiveness and receive Your love. Thank You for walking with me each day and making Yourself more and more real to me. In Jesus' name I pray.

Amen!

Chapter 11

KEVIN HAS THE LAST WORD

IN THIS CHAPTER, I WANTED to let Kevin have the words. He had written some poems and thoughts in his teenage years that range from thought provoking to just funny. It will give you a glimpse into the kind of person Kevin was. They are precious treasures to me and I wanted to share them with you. I would also like to invite you to visit his Facebook Wall to look at the albums of photos of Kevin living life.
 https://www.facebook.com/kevinsunshineyates
ENJOY!

CHOICES

KEVIN DANIEL YATES

K ind

E ver loving

V enturous

I maginative

N ever ending fun

D estined to play the trumpet

A lways laughing

N ever ending love

I ntelligent

E asy loving friend

L oving

Y ounger brother

A lways fun

T ell you my true feelings

E verlasting fun

S atisfied with GOD

LOVE

Love keeps on trusting God even when the right choices you make don't turn out the way you want.

Love keeps on expecting the best from God; not yourself.

Love doesn't give up just because something goes wrong or because your feelings are hurt.

Love doesn't keep thinking over and over again about how someone hurt you.

Love lets others have their turn talking.

Love isn't stuck up.

Love is willing to wait.

SOAR

The words in His book are messages for your deliverance.

The only thing that can hold you back is <u>your</u> resistance.

You have manuals for almost everything.

Well, God's got one too.

The Bible is His Word and manual.

If you don't read it you may die.

If you don't read a manual for a plane,

You'll never be able to fly.

But if you don't read God's manual,

You won't see the golden streets.

But if you do you can soar forever.

THE SWEET, SWEET LOVE OF GOD

The love of God is such a sweet love.

This love will fit with you like a hand and a glove.

He gives it to you so you don't feel alone.

He wants you to have this love for your own.

You have someone that loves you,

But God loves you more,

Because He has the love that will endure.

His love will stay with you forever and ever.

It will go with this, that, and whatever.

His love will forgive and understands your mistakes,

Because you will have more than one mistake.

God's love will not disappear with the blink of an eye,

Because He has the love that doesn't say goodbye.

He gave His life because His love is so strong.

He's got the love that will never be wrong.

If one other love will put nails in its wrist and hang on a cross,

God's love will still go further and come back for the lost.

LESS IS MORE

More of Him and less of me,

That's the way it's supposed to be.

Fasting and praying and the Holy Spirit too,

These are the things we are supposed to have and do.

Take a drink of His blood and a bite of His flesh.

This is what I have on my plate.

God is what should be on your plate.

The Trinity is whom I call my Soulmate.

More of Him and less of me,

Then God turns on the light so you can see.

A life with God is so eternal.

Stick with Him and your walk won't have a fall.

So give God your life and He'll give you His.

Since God is your target you cannot miss.

If you're living with God, there is no fee,

Except more of Him and less of me.

BIBLE

This book is my B-I-B-L-E

This is the book that helps me see.

This is the book that has saved me.

This is the only B-I-B-L-E

This is the book that set me free

This book was made by the big G

If something's not from this book it's from the little g

Reading this book shall show the way to the big G

So if I were you I'd be reading my B-I-B-L-E.

RESPECT

My definition of respect is to be polite to others and being honest. It is to show consideration to others when around them. Respect is to appreciate others and to do as they ask of you as long as it's right. You also have to be truthful to them. People will respect and pay attention to you if you give them respect. If you respect someone you should be quiet while they are on the phone and especially while they are sleeping. You should respect people's rights if you would like people to respect your rights too. The people that you should respect are your Mom and Daddy, your brothers and your sisters, your Grandparents, and all of your other relatives. You should also respect your Teachers and anyone else that might be in charge or responsible for you. And most of all you should respect God.

KEVIN HAS THE LAST WORD

PAIN

What is this I feel in me, There's a blankness no one knows.
A hole that only I can see, That pain is my life.

Everything I do is wrong, No one understands it.
It gets stronger all day long. That pain is my life.

You try to understand, I don't know if I can trust.
Now every time "I lay me down to sleep" and go to bed,
That pain is my life.

Darkness all around I don't know what to do!
Everythng must surround That pain is my life.

I fall to my knees with my hand cringing in my hair
...........AAAHHHHHHHHHHHHHHHHH!!!!!
Everything comes and I'm unable to bear
That pain is my life. One man was made to save me
There is no possible way How can this be? " JESUS!!!"......the pain is gone.

CHOICES

__BE ASSURED__

I can see them down below me

Some laugh but they want to cry

But not a single one can see

The question they repeatedly ask, WHY?

A river of blood is flowing from my wrists

The pain from the stripes on my back

After the storm, I die in the mist

But be assured, I will come back.

After three days they had to see to believe,

That I have come back again

Trust came back to those that deceived

And forgiveness given to those in sin.

I go away again

But when I come back

I'm coming for my children

But be assured, I will come back.

PRESSURE

You get pressured by everyone.

You hear it all the time.

"He's coming back for us."

You cannot be blind.

Don't look in the past.

Look toward the goal.

Straighten up your life

Or you'll get left behind.

He will come back,

But maybe not in your lifetime,

But still you should set the example,

So you won't have to follow.

You need to be a leader.

Show the next generation where to go,

Cause if you don't

It's your fault they're barbecue!

CHOICES

FAST

We are on a 50 day fast

and I left thinking; how long could it last.

But every time I come to a feast

I get a temptation from the beast

Cookies, chocolate, and brownies too

so many sweets; what should I do

It's only one time, so He'll understand.

He will stay with me hand in hand.

When I get home there's the TV

it's so hard to fast you see.

I go to my room and see the 64

so many things; should I say more.

TV and sweets, video games and meats.

It's so hard; I can't do it on my own.

Please tell me Lord, I have to be shown.

Then God said, "You've finally realized the truth of the fast.

Believe in Me or you won't last,

Give Me your life and I'll set you free

It truly is easy; don't you see?"

KEVIN HAS THE LAST WORD

GOD

God is love, God is power,

God is sweet, never sour.

God is peace, he is patience,

He's a bright light, never dim.

God is grateful, God is sweet,

He is my bread, He is my meat.

God is meekness, God is kind,

God is endlessly on my mind.

God is my provider, God is in my heart.

He is in the beginning and at the start.

He is with me, He is with you.

God had saved me so He'll save you too.

Thanks for taking the time to read Kevin's words. It means a lot to me.

About the Author

Written by Tiki's son and 1N3 cofounder, Derek Yates.

So my mom, Tiki Rene' Finlayson, is one of the strongest, not only women, but people I know. She's been through hell and back, yet she continues pressing on despite all that life has sent her way. Most people might only experience one of the events my mom has had to go through, yet she's gone through multiple, including the loss of her baby boy through a tragic situation.

Throughout it all, she's held her head high even as the tears come streaming down. Through those tears she continues looking forward. Through those tears she has chosen to use her pain and suffering to impact the lives around her in hopes of saving even just one person so that no one else would have to go through anything like what she's had to experience.

And despite so much, by deciding to share her story to change the minds of those who will listen, she became the driving force behind the forgiveness that pretty much everyone affected by Kevin's death came to have towards the woman who killed him. She also extended her love and help towards the woman, knowing she was going through her own form of pain and suffering. If that isn't strength, then I do not know what is.

Her strength has affected me and taught me so much in my own life. I've learned to fight for what I want and never give up. That resilience has helped me continue pushing for the dreams and goals I have for my life and, of course, has helped to equip me with what I've needed to process the death of my brother. And as life inevitably ends for us all, it will help me through future losses to come as well.

I hope this opportunity to hear her story has empowered and encourage you as it has for so many others. ~Derek Yates

Tiki's story has been featured by the BBC, DailyMail.com, YouMatter (Part 1 & Part 2), and BVOV, just to name a few . She has won awards such as Volunteer Advocate of the Year, Voice for Victims, and Recognition of Inspiration. She has spent years inspiring and motivating audiences to make better choices that will impact their future in a positive way. Tiki has spoken at a wide variety of events, schools, churches, rehabilitation centers, and correctional facilities along with many others. She is now in the process of completing her first book about her journey of forgiveness and how choices matter.

Tiki was born and raised in Chattanooga, TN. After living in many different places she decided to move back and now resides there. She is a wife, mother of four, Gigi to three grandchildren, a co-founder of two nonprofits, 1N3 and Pursuing Purpose (PPM), a pastor of Purpose Church alongside her husband, Tom, and a Donate Life Ambassador. She has been trained and educated by the "University of Hard Knocks". After many ups and downs she decided to use what she had learned to help others through mentoring and speaking engagements.

www.tikifinlayson.com

FOLLOW ME ON SOCIAL MEDIA
www.facebook.com/tikifinlayson
www.twitter.com/tikifinlayson
www.instagram.com/tikifinlayson

Acknowledgments

I am so overwhelmed by the number of people who came together and help make possible this book you are holding in your hand. Thank you just doesn't seem to be enough. I could not have published this book without each of them.

I also want to say a special "thank you" to three people. To my husband, Tom, for sacrificing his Tiki time with me during my seven years of writing of this book, and for holding me when reliving this horrible tragedy over and over as the words came out and became a book. To my oldest son, Derek, for his support, input and advice as well as his creative ability on this project, I would not have wanted to complete this book without him. To my Mom, Rene', for ALWAYS being by my side and cheering me on through this life, thank you all for believing in me and encouraging me to finish writing my book.

Contributors

Listed alphabetically

Alicia Hill	ripple story
Amber Bell	launch team
Arthur Marroquin	author headshot (ABM Photography)
Casey Brostek	ripple story
Cassie Stone	ripple story, launch team
Christy Seepe	launch team
Crystal Richards	ripple story, launch team
Darlene Underwood	proofreader, publishing consultant
Dawn Benjamin	editor, proofreader, consultant
Dene Sims	launch team
Derek Yates	book cover, website (Derek Yates Photography)
Faye Duffy	launch team
Gerard Flores	marketing consultant
Gina Griffin	message from Kevin
Jenny Klein	launch team
Katie Hendrix	proofreader
Larry Benz	editor
Latisha Stephens	ripple story
Lisa Fairbanks	proofreader, launch team
Melvin Ellis	ripple story, Kevin's heart recipient
Natalie Leibold	launch team
Patty Boyd	launch team
Paula Harlow	proofreader, formatting, launch team
Rene' Bell	ripple story, launch team
Talisa Walker	ripple story
Tom Finlayson	gave up Tiki time so I could write
Valerie Sinclair	proofreader

Thanks for reading! Please add a short review on Amazon and let me know what you thought!

NOTES

NOTES

NOTES

NOTES